Let's Learn Japanese
with Hiragana and Katakana

I0644904

Let's Learn Japanese with Hiragana and Katakana

By

Masumi Kai

Illustrations by Ms. Yi-Wei Chiu

CAMBRIDGE
SCHOLARS
PUBLISHING

Let's Learn Japanese with Hiragana and Katakana,
by Masumi Kai

This book first published 2013

Cambridge Scholars Publishing

12 Back Chapman Street, Newcastle upon Tyne, NE6 2XX, UK

British Library Cataloguing in Publication Data
A catalogue record for this book is available from the British Library

Copyright © 2013 by Masumi Kai

All rights for this book reserved. No part of this book may be reproduced, stored in a retrieval system, or transmitted, in any form or by any means, electronic, mechanical, photocopying, recording or otherwise, without the prior permission of the copyright owner.

ISBN (10): 1-4438-4659-7, ISBN (13): 978-1-4438-4659-2

TABLE OF CONTENTS

Part One: Hiragana Practice ひらがな れんしゅう

Part Two: Katakana Practice カタカナ れんしゅう

Acknowledgements

This book was published with the support of a grant from the University of Guam.

PART ONE:

HIRAGANA PRACTICE ひらがな れんしゅう

Japanese Characters

History of Japanese characters:

The Japanese language has three kinds of characters; hiragana, katakana and kanji. The Chinese character, kanji, was brought from China. It is thought to have been introduced around the third or fourth century, although this has not been proved. Kanji, which is an ideogram character (to represent meanings), started to be used as a phonogram (to represent sounds) called *Manyo-kana*. As kanji became more widely used, it was simplified. This simplified form became hiragana. Hiragana has a roundish shape as shown below, and it was considered to be the letters for private use and female use.

ex. 安→あ　　以→い　　加→か

Japanese word order and Chinese word order are different. Small size kanji (*kun'ten*) were placed next to kanji to indicate the Japanese word order when reading classical Chinese. Then it was simplified and became katakana. Many katakana were made from a part of kanji as seen below. Katakana has rather straight lines.

ex. 阿→ア　　伊→イ　　加→カ

不レ足下為二外人一道上也

example of *kun'ten*

How to use the three kinds of characters:

The three kinds of characters are used in different ways. Normally katakana is used for loanwords and foreign names like *koohii* (coffee) or *nyuuyooku* (New York). Most content words are written using kanji. Functional words like *desu* (to be), particles, and some Japanese origin words like *oishii* (tasty) are written in hiragana. All three characters can be used in one sentence like below.

ex.	彼	は	ミラー	さん	です。
	kanji 'he'	hiragana topic marker	katakana 'Miller'	hiragana 'Mr.'	hiragana 'is'

'He is Mr. Miller.'

Japanese period and comma:

The Japanese language uses a *maru* (circle) at the end of sentences and *ten* (dot) for semantic separation in a sentence. Traditionally Japanese does not use the question mark "?" for an interrogative sentence. Unlike English there is no space between words. Instead a combination of the three kinds of characters can indicate if it is a meaning word, a foreign word, or a functional word.

ex. 明日の朝、トムさんに会います。

tomorrow of morning Tom Mr. with meet

'Tomorrow morning, (I) will meet Tom.'

Roma-ji:

Roma-ji (romanized Japanese) is used to indicate the pronunciation of hiragana and katakana in this book. There are two types of roma-ji; *Hebon* system and Japanese system. Most are spelled the same, but a few are spelled differently. Even though they are spelled differently, their pronunciations are the same. This textbook uses the *Hebon* system.

Hebon system	shi	chi	fu	sha	shu	sho	ja	ji	ju	jo
Japanese system	si	ti	hu	sya	syu	syo	zya	zi	zyu	zyo

Font type:

As in English, Japanese has several font types, some of which are a bit different. Below are examples.

ex. き=き さ=さ そ=そ ふ=ふ/ふ ら=ら り=り や=や

Stroke end:

There are three features at the stroke ends of hiragana, katakana, and kanji. One is *tome* (stop), the second is *hane* (jump), and the third is *harai* (sweep).

ex.

BASIC SOUNDS ♪♫

	a	i	u	e	o
	あ a	い i	う u	え e	お o
k	か ka	き ki	く ku	け ke	こ ko
s	さ sa	し **shi**	す su	せ se	そ so
t	た ta	ち **chi**	つ **tsu**	て te	と to
n	な na	に ni	ぬ nu	ね ne	の no
h	は ha	ひ hi	ふ fu	へ he	ほ ho
m	ま ma	み mi	む mu	め me	も mo
y	や ya	(い)	ゆ yu	(え)	よ yo
r	ら ra	り ri	る ru	れ re	ろ ro
w	わ wa	(い)	(う)	(え)	を wo (=o)
N	ん n				

VOICED SOUNDS AND P-SOUNDS

	a	i	u	e	o
g	が ga	ぎ gi	ぐ gu	げ ge	ご go
z	ざ za	じ **ji**	ず **zu**	ぜ ze	ぞ zo
d	だ da	ぢ **ji**	づ **zu**	で de	ど do
b	ば ba	び bi	ぶ bu	べ be	ぼ bo
p	ぱ pa	ぴ pi	ぷ pu	ぺ pe	ぽ po

Y-SOUNDS

	a	u	o
ky	きゃ kya	きゅ kyu	きょ kyo
gy	ぎゃ gya	ぎゅ gyu	ぎょ gyo
sh	しゃ sha	しゅ shu	しょ sho
j	じゃ ja	じゅ ju	じょ jo
ch	ちゃ cha	ちゅ chu	ちょ cho
ny	にゃ nya	にゅ nyu	にょ nyo
hy	ひゃ hya	ひゅ hyu	ひょ hyo
by	びゃ bya	びゅ byu	びょ byo
my	みゃ mya	みゅ myu	みょ myo
ry	りゃ rya	りゅ ryu	りょ ryo
py	ぴゃ pya	ぴゅ pyu	ぴょ pyo

Listen to CD Lesson 1 for the sounds and the stroke order.

PRACTICE WRITING

a **to** *o*

あ	a	あ	あ	あ	あ		
い	i	い	い	い	い		
う	u	う	う	う	う		
え	e	え	え	え	え		
お	o	お	お	お	お		

What is wrong?

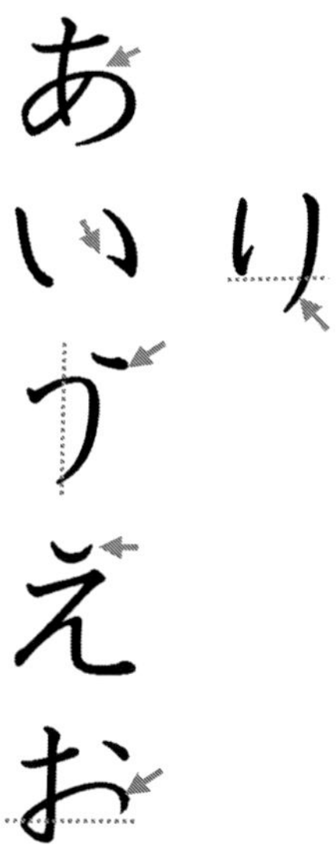

Let's read and write!

あおい

blue

あ	お	い

うえ

above

う	え

え

painting

え

いえ

house

い	え

Now you can write words using hiragana. Let's try.

1) blue painting

あ	お	い	え
a	o	i	e

2) blue house

あ	お	い	い	え
a	o	i	i	e

What is wrong?

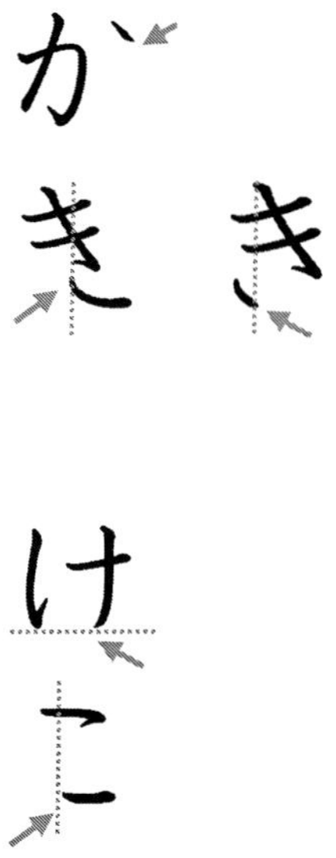

ka* to *ko

か	ka	か	か	か	か		
き	ki	き	き	き	き		
く	ku	く	く	く	く		
け	ke	け	け	け	け		
こ	ko	こ	こ	こ	こ		

Let's read and write!

あかい

red

あ	か	い

えき

station

え	き

き

tree/wood

き

いけ

pond

い	け

ここ

here

こ	こ

Let's write a sentence.

In the sentence below, は (*wa*) is a topic marker meaning 'as far as', and です(*desu*) corresponds to 'is' in English. は is read as 'wa' when it is used as a topic marker. The Japanese period is a small circle '。' at the lower left hand corner. Note that the Japanese word order is 'Topic は noun です。'. Also notice that the Japanese word order is 'Topic は noun です。'.

1) (You are showing your friend around town)
Here is the station.

こ	こ	は	え	き	で	す	。
ko	ko	wa	e	ki	de	su	

Now try CD L2 part 1 & L3 part 1.

sa* to *so

さ	sa	さ	さ	さ	さ		
し	shi	し	し	し	し		
す	su	す	す	す	す		
せ	se	せ	せ	せ	せ		
そ	so	そ	そ	そ	そ		

What is wrong?

Let's read and write!

かさ

umbrella

か さ

おさけ

alcohol

お さ け

いす

chair

い す

せ

height

せ

そこ

there

そ こ

Let's write words.

In the second set of words below, の (*no*) is a connector between two nouns.

1) red umbrella

あ	か	い	か	さ
a	ka	i	ka	sa

2) wood chair

き	の	い	す
ki	no	i	su

ta* to *to

た	ta	た	た	た	た		
ち	chi	ち	ち	ち	ち		
つ	tsu	つ	つ	つ	つ		
て	te	て	て	て	て		
と	to	と	と	と	と		

What is wrong?

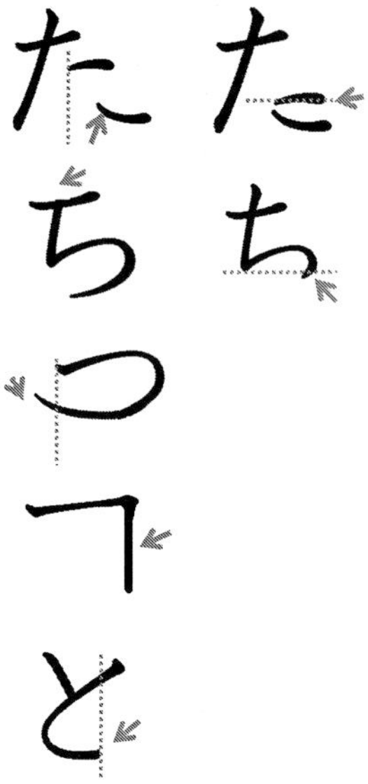

Let's read and write!

たかい

high/expensive

た	か	い

ちかてつ

subway

ち	か	て	つ

つくえ

desk

つ	く	え

て

hand

て

そと

outside

そ	と

した

below/under

し	た

くつ

shoes

く	つ

Let's write words.

In the second set of words below, be aware that つくえ(*tsukue*) 'desk' comes first in Japanese, and の (*no*) is a connecter between two nouns.

1) expensive shoes

た	か	い	く	つ
ta	ka	i	ku	tsu

2) under the desk

つ	く	え	の	し	た
tsu	ku	e	no	shi	su

➡ Now try CD L2 part 2 & L3 part 2.

na* to *no

な	na	な	な	な	な		
に	ni	に	に	に	に		
ぬ	nu	ぬ	ぬ	ぬ	ぬ		
ね	ne	ね	ね	ね	ね		
の	no	の	の	の	の		

What is wrong?

な な
に
ぬ ぬ
ね
の

Let's read and write!

あなた

You

あ	な	た

さかな

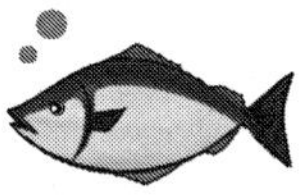

fish

さ	か	な

くに

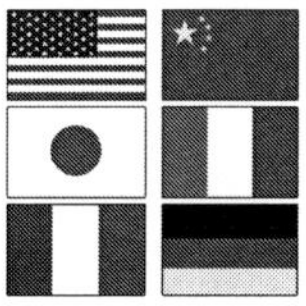

country

く	に

いぬ

dog

い	ぬ

ねこ

cat

ね	こ

この

this

こ	の

Let's write words.

1) your dog

あ	な	た	の	い	ぬ
a	na	ta	no	i	nu

2) this cat

こ	の	ね	こ
ko	no	ne	ko

ha to *ho*

は	ha	は	は	は	は		
ひ	hi	ひ	ひ	ひ	ひ		
ふ	fu	ふ	ふ	ふ	ふ		
へ	he	へ	へ	へ	へ		
ほ	ho	ほ	ほ	ほ	ほ		

What is wrong?

Let's read and write!

はこ

box

は	こ

ひと

person

ひ	と

さいふ

wallet

さ	い	ふ

へた

be poor at

へ	た

ほし

star

ほ	し

Let's write a word and a sentence.

In the second sentence below, be aware that the Japanese period is a small circle.

1) this person

こ	の	ひ	と
ko	no	hi	to

2) (I) am poor at (something).

へ	た	で	す	。
he	ta	de	su	

Now try CD L2 part 3 & L3 part 3.

What is wrong?

ma* to *mo

ま	ma	ま	ま	ま	ま		
み	mi	み	み	み	み		
む	mu	む	む	む	む		
め	me	め	め	め	め		
も	mo	も	も	も	も		

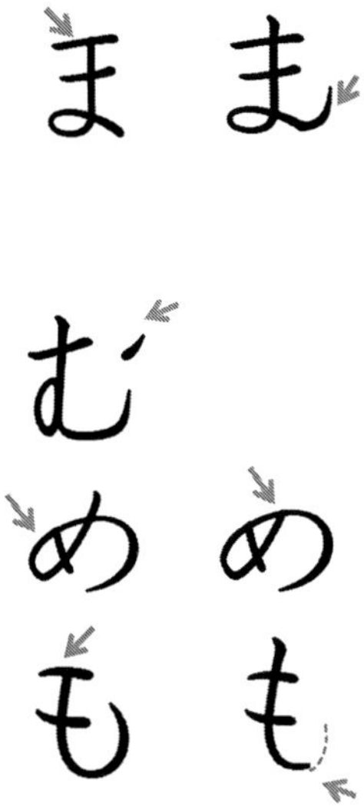

Let's read and write!

なまえ

name

な	ま	え

うみ

ocean

う	み

むすめ

daughter

む	す	め

あめ

rain

あ	め

もも

peach

も	も

かきます

to write/ to draw

か	き	ま	す

まち

town/big city

ま	ち

Let's write words.

1) daughter's name

む	す	め	の	な	ま	え
mu	su	me	no	na	ma	e

2) blue ocean

あ	お	い	う	み
a	o	i	u	mi

ya* to *yo

や	ya	①②③ や	や	や	や		
ゆ	yu	①② ゆ	ゆ	ゆ	ゆ		
よ	yo	①② よ	よ	よ	よ		

What is wrong?

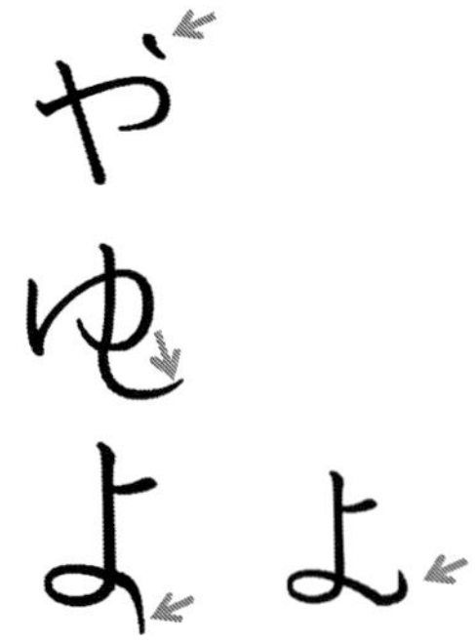

Let's read and write!

やま

mountain

や	ま

ゆき

snow

ゆ	き

よみます

to read

よ	み	ま	す

へや

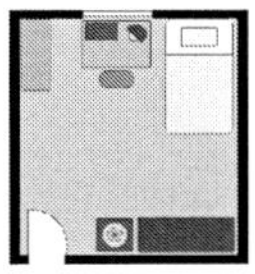

room

へ	や

Let's write a word.

1) mountain snow

や	ま	の	ゆ	き
ya	ma	no	yu	ki

2) high mountain

た	か	い	や	ま
ta	ka	i	ya	ma

Now try CD L2 part 4 & L3 part 4.

What is wrong?

ra* to *ro

ら	ra	ら	ら	ら	ら		
り	ri	り	り	り	り		
る	ru	る	る	る	る		
れ	re	れ	れ	れ	れ		
ろ	ro	ろ	ろ	ろ	ろ		

ら
り
る
れ
ろ

Let's read and write!

おてら

temple

くすり

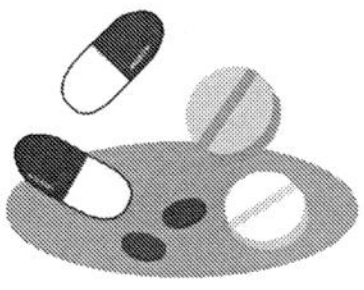

medicine

はる

spring

はれ

clear sky

しろい

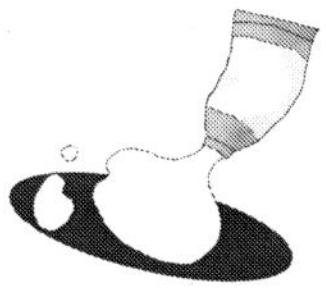

white

お	て	ら	く	す	り	は	る	は	れ	し	ろ	い	

Let's write words.

In the first set of words below, be aware that はる (*haru*) 'spring' comes first in Japanese, and の (*no*) is a connecter between two nouns. In the second set of words, と (*to*) means 'and' in English and connects nouns.

1) temple in Spring

は	る	の	お	て	ら
ha	ru	no	o	te	ra

2) white medicine and blue medicine

し	ろ	い	く	す	り	と	あ	お	い	く	す	り
shi	ro	i	ku	su	ri	to	a	o	i	ku	su	ri

What is wrong?

wa* to *n

わ	wa	わ	わ	わ	わ			
を	wo	を	を	を	を			
ん	n	ん	ん	ん	ん			

Let's read and write!

わたし

I

わ | た | し

かわ

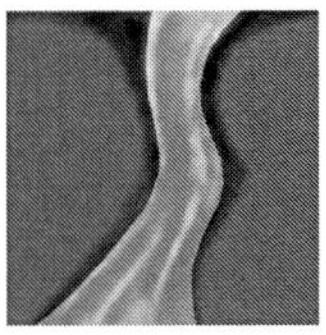

river

か | わ

なまえをかきます

to write a name

な | ま | え | を | か | き | ま | す

ほん

book

ほ | ん

にほん

Japan

に | ほ | ん

せんもん

major

せ | ん | も | ん

しけん

exam

し | け | ん

Let's write a sentence.

In the second sentence below, を (*wo*) is a particle attached to an object noun. In this case ほん (*hon*) 'book is an object noun. よみます (*yomimasu*) means 'to read'. Japanese word order is Topic-Object-Verb.

1) my major

わ	た	し	の	せ	ん	も	ん
wa	ta	shi	no	se	n	mo	n

2) I read a book.

わ	た	し	は	ほ	ん	を	よ	み	ま	す	。
wa	ta	shi	wa	ho	n	wo	yo	mi	ma	su	

Now try CD L2 part 5 & L3 part 5.

VOICED SOUNDS AND P-SOUNDS

Voiced sounds are indicated by basic hiragana with *tenten* (two short lines on top).

ga* to *go

が	ぎ	ぐ	げ	ご
ga	gi	gu	ge	go

Let's read and write!

まんが

comic

おんがく

music

かぎ

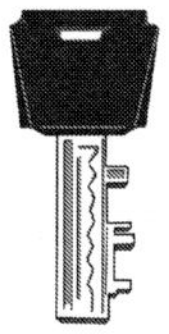

key

かぐ

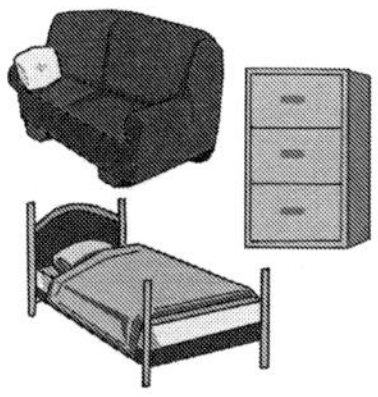

furniture

ま	ん	が

お	ん	が	く

か	ぎ

か	ぐ

おみやげ

souvenir

にほんご

Japanese language

ごご

afternoon/PM

お	み	や	げ

に	ほ	ん	ご

ご	ご

Let's write words.

1) Japanese magazine (a magazine written in the Japanese language)

に	ほ	ん	ご	の	ま	ん	が
ni	ho	n	go	no	ma	n	ga

2) Japanese souvenir (a souvenir from a trip to Japan)

に	ほ	ん	の	お	み	や	げ
ni	ho	n	no	o	mi	ya	ge

za* to *zo

ざ	じ	ず	ぜ	ぞ
za	ji	zu	ze	zo

Let's read and write!

かんざし

hair clip

か	ん	ざ	し

かんじ

kanji

か	ん	じ

ちず

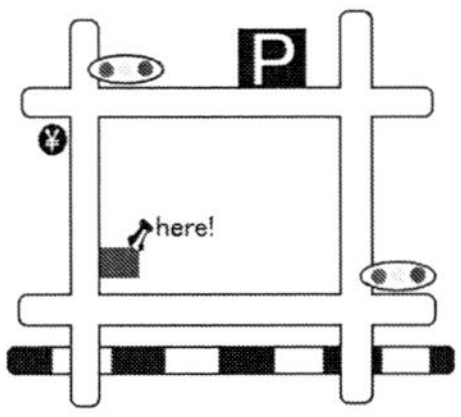

map

ち	ず

みず

water

み	ず

ごぜん

AM

ご	ぜ	ん

かぞく

family

か	ぞ	く

Let's write a sentence.

1) I write kanji.

わ	た	し	は	か	ん	じ	を	か	き	ま	す	。
wa	ta	shi	wa	ka	n	ji	wo	ka	ki	ma	su	

Now try CD L3 part 6.

da* to *do

だ	ぢ	づ	で	ど
da	ji	zu	de	do

Let's read and write!

だいがく

university

だ	い	が	く

ともだち

friend

と	も	だ	ち

はなぢ

bloody nose

は	な	ぢ

みかづき

crescent moon

み	か	づ	き

でんわ

telephone

で	ん	わ

どこ

where

ど	こ

こども

child

こ	ど	も

Let's write a sentence.

In the sentence below, か (*ka*) is a question marker attached to the end of the question sentence. Be aware that the Japanese word order is 'telephone-where-is'.

1) Where is the telephone?

で	ん	わ	は	ど	こ	で	す	か	。
de	n	wa	wa	do	ko	de	su	ka	

ba* to *bo

ば	び	ぶ	べ	ぼ
ba	bi	bu	be	bo

Let's read and write!

かばん

bag

か	ば	ん

えび

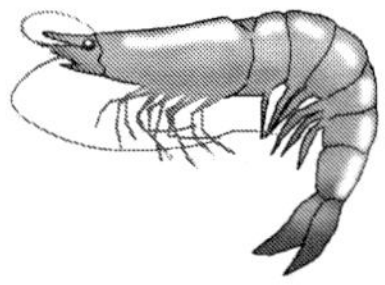

shrimp

え	び

しんぶん

news paper

し	ん	ぶ	ん

たべます

to eat

た	べ	ま	す

たんぼ

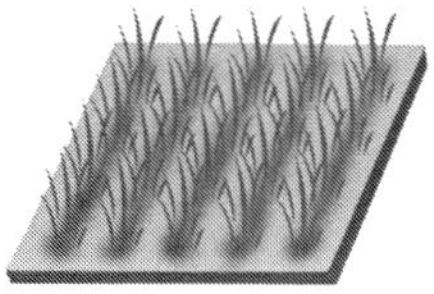

rice field

た	ん	ぼ

Let's write a sentence.

1) I read a newspaper.

わ	た	し	は	し	ん	ぶ	ん	を	よ	み	ま	す	。
wa	ta	shi	wa	shi	n	bu	n	wo	yo	mi	ma	su	

➡ Now try CD L3 part 7.

pa* to *po

ぱ	ぴ	ぷ	ぺ	ぽ
pa	pi	pu	pe	po

Let's read and write!

かんぱい

toast

えんぴつ

pencil

さんぷん

three minutes

か	ん	ぱ	い

え	ん	ぴ	つ

さ	ん	ぷ	ん

*ぺんぎん

Note: This word is usually written in katakana.

penguin

たんぽぽ

dandelion

ぺ	ん	ぎ	ん

た	ん	ぽ	ぽ

Let's write a sentence.

In the sentence below, かいます (*kaimasu*) means 'to buy'.

1) I buy a pencil.

わ	た	し	は	え	ん	ぴ	つ	を	か	い	ま	す	。
wa	ta	shi	wa	e	n	pi	tsu	wo	ka	i	ma	su	

Now try CD L3 part 8 and L4 part 1 to part 6.

Stopped Sounds

Stopped sounds are indicated by small ‘つ’ (tsu). ‘つ’ is quarter size.

つ	

Let’s read and write!

がっき

musical instrument

が	っ	き

きっぷ

(transportation) ticket

き	っ	ぷ

きって

stamp

き	っ	て

きっさてん

coffee shop/cafe

き	っ	さ	て	ん

ざっし

magazine

ざ	っ	し

Let’s write a sentence.

In the second sentence below, ひきます (*hikimasu*) means ‘to play (musical instrument)’.

1) (I) buy a stamp.

き	っ	て	を	か	い	ま	す	。
ki		tte	wo	ka	i	ma	su	

2) I play a musical instrument.

わ	た	し	は	が	っ	き	を	ひ	き	ま	す	。
wa	ta	shi	wa	ga		kki	wo	hi	ki	ma	su	

➡ Now try CD L4 part 7.

Long Vowels

Let's read and write!

aa (a:): add 'あ'.

おかあさん 

mother

おばあさん 

grandmother

お	か	あ	さ	ん

お	ば	あ	さ	ん

ii (i:) : add 'い'.

おにいさん 

older brother

おじいさん 

grandfather

お	に	い	さ	ん

お	じ	い	さ	ん

uu (u:) : add 'う'.

ふうせん

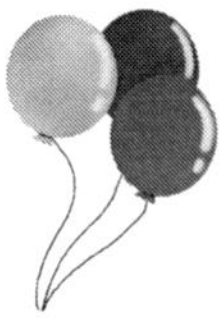

balloon

すうがく

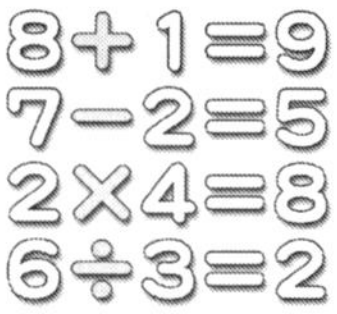

mathematics

こうえん

park

ふ	う	せ	ん

す	う	が	く

こ	う	え	ん

ee (e:) : add 'い'.

とけい

clock/watch

がくせい

student

えいご

English

おね<u>え</u>さん

exception!

older sister

と	け	い

が	く	せ	い

え	い	ご

お	ね	え	さ	ん

oo (o:) : add ‘う’, but some exceptions add ‘お’.

ぼうし ぎんこう おとうさん おとうと いもうと

hat/cap

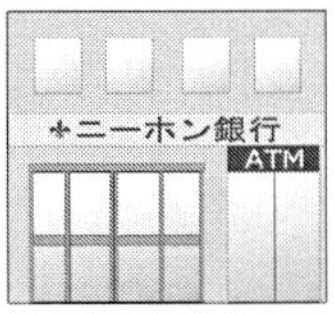

bank

father

younger brother

younger sister

ぼ	う	し

ぎ	ん	こ	う

お	と	う	さ	ん

お	と	う	と

い	も	う	と

おおさか

Osaka

おおきい

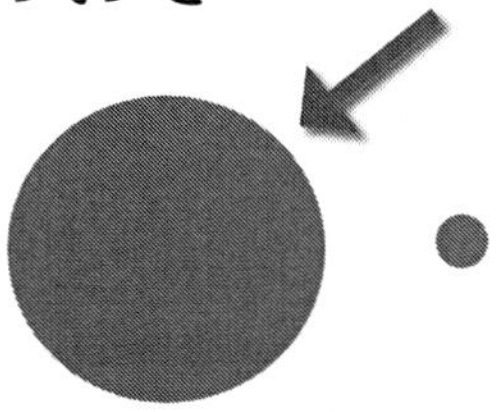

big

とおい

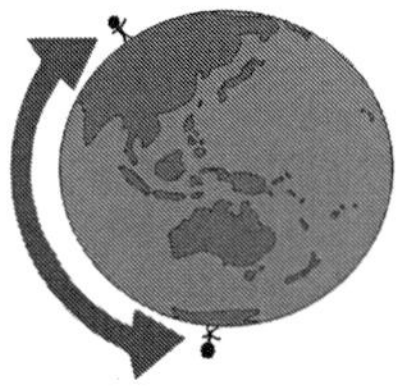

far

こおり

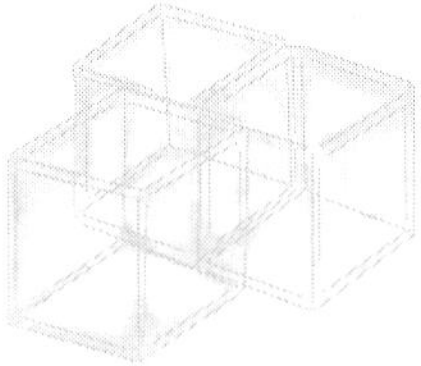

ice

お	お	さ	か

お	お	き	い

と	お	い

こ	お	り

Let’s write a sentence.

1) My younger sister is a student.

わ	た	し	の	い	も	う	と	は	が	く	せ	い	で	す	。
wa	ta	shi	no	i	mo	o	to	wa	ga	ku	se	e	de	su	

Now try CD L4 part 8.

Y-SOUNDS

Consonants k, s, t, n, h, m, r, g, z, b have Y-sounds. Y sounds consist of a consonant plus '-ya', '-yu', '-yo'. 'や', 'ゆ', 'よ' are quarter size.

きゃ	きゅ	きょ
kya	kyu	kyo

Let's read and write!

きゃく

guest

き	ゃ	く

ちきゅう

earth

ち	き	ゅ	う

きょうかい

church

き	ょ	う	か	い

ぎゃ	ぎゅ	ぎょ
gya	gyu	gyo

Let's read and write!

ぎゃく

opposite

ぎ	ゃ	く

ぎゅうにく

beef

ぎ	ゅ	う	に	く

きんぎょ

goldfish

き	ん	ぎ	ょ

Let's write a sentence.

In the sentence below, いきます (*ikimasu*) is 'to go'. You need the particle に (*ni*) after a destination. In this case きょうかい (*kyookai*) 'church' is a destination.

1) I go to a church.

わ	た	し	は	き	ょ	う	か	い	に	い	き	ま	す	。
wa	ta	shi	wa	kyo		o	ka	i	ni	i	ki	ma	su	

しゃ	しゅ	しょ
sha	shu	sho

Let's read and write!

かいしゃ　しゅくだい　きょうかしょ　としょかん

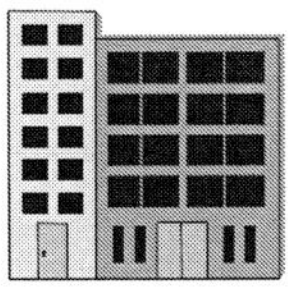

company

homework

textbook

library

か	い	し	ゃ

し	ゅ	く	だ	い

き	ょ	う	か	し	ょ

と	し	ょ	か	ん

Let's write a sentence.
In the sentence below, します (*shimasu*) is 'to do'.

1) I do (my) homework.

わ	た	し	は	し	ゅ	く	だ	い	を	し	ま	す	。
wa	ta	shi	wa	shu		ku	da	i	wo	shi	ma	su	

じゃ	じゅ	じょ
ja	ju	jo

Let's read and write!

じゃんけん　じゅうどう　きんじょ

rock/paper/scissors

judo

neighborhood

じ	ゃ	ん	け	ん

じ	ゅ	う	ど	う

き	ん	じ	ょ

ちゃ	ちゅ	ちょ
cha	chu	cho

Let's read and write!

おちゃ

tea

ちゅうごく

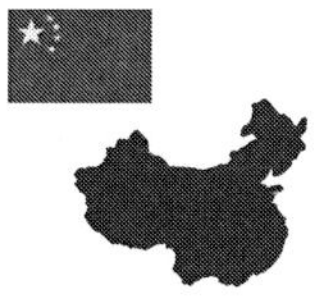

China

ちょっと

a minute/a bit

お	ち	ゃ

ち	ゅ	う	ご	く

ち	ょ	っ	と

にゃ	にゅ	にょ
nya	nyu	nyo

Let's read and write!

にゃあにゃあ

howling sounds of a cat

ぎゅうにゅう

milk

にょきにょき

situation where a plant grows quickly

に	ゃ	あ	に	ゃ	あ

ぎ	ゅ	う	に	ゅ	う

に	ょ	き	に	ょ	き

Let's write a sentence.

In the sentence below, のみます (*nomimasu*) is 'to drink'. と (*to*) means 'and'.

1) (I) drink tea and milk.

お	ち	ゃ	と	ぎ	ゅ	う	に	ゅ	う	を	の	み	ま	す	。

o cha to gyu u nyu u wo no mi ma su

ひゃ	ひゅ	ひょ
hya	hyu	hyo

Let's read and write!

ひゃく

100

a hundred

ひゅうひゅう

the sound of the wind blowing

ひょう

table/chart

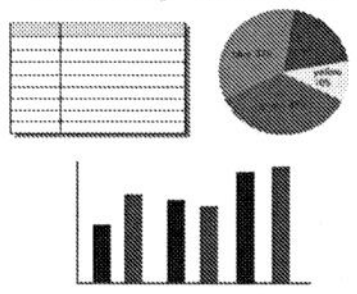

table/chart

ひ	ゃ	く

ひ	ゅ	う	ひ	ゅ	う

ひ	ょ	う

びゃ	びゅ	びょ
bya	byu	byo

Let's read and write!

さんびゃく

300

three hundred

びゅうびゅう

sound of a strong wind 'to zip'

びょういん

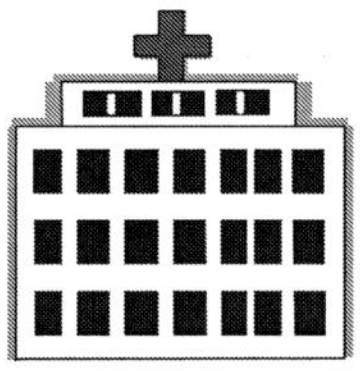

hospital

さ	ん	び	ゃ	く

び	ゅ	う	び	ゅ	う

び	ょ	う	い	ん

Let's write a sentence.

1) I go to the hospital.

わ	た	し	は	び	ょ	う	い	ん	に	い	き	ま	す	。
wa	ta	shi	wa	byo		o	i	n	ni	i	ki	ma	su	

ぴゃ	ぴゅ	ぴょ
pya	pyu	pyo

Let's read and write!

ろっぴゃく

six hundred

ぴゅっと

a quick movement, like water or train

ぴょこぴょこ（あるく）

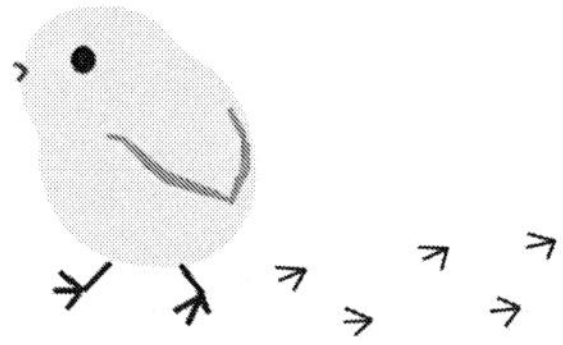

a way of walking like a chick or a small child

ろ	っ	ぴ	ゃ	く

ぴ	ゅ	っ	と

ぴ	ょ	こ	ぴ	ょ	こ

みゃ	みゅ	みょ
mya	myu	myo

Let's read and write!

みゃく

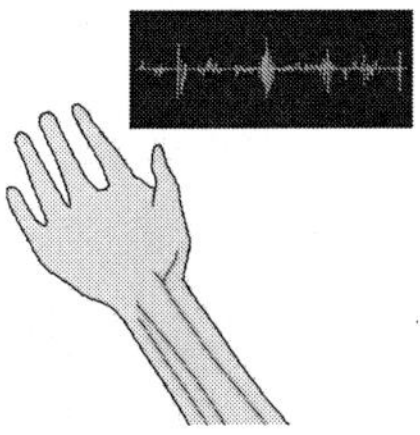

pulse

*みゅうじかる

musical

Note: This word is usually written in katakana.

みょうじ

last name (family name)

み	ゃ	く

み	ゅ	う	じ	か	る

み	ょ	う	じ

Let's write a sentence.

1) My family name is Tanaka.

わ	た	し	の	み	ょ	う	じ	は	た	な	か	で	す	。
wa	ta	shi	no	myo		o	ji	wa	ta	na	ka	de	su	

りゃ	りゅ	りょ
rya	ryu	ryo

Let's read and write!

しょうりゃく

パーソナル
コンピュータ
↓
パソコン

omission

りゅうがくせい

International Student

りょこう

trip

し	ょ	う	り	ゃ	く

り	ゅ	う	が	く	せ	い

り	ょ	こ	う

Let's write a sentence.

In the sentence below, かのじょ (*kanojo*) is 'she' and からきました (*kara kimashita*) means 'came from'.

1) Ms. Noriko is an international student. She came from Japan.

の	り	こ	さ	ん	は	り	ゅ	う	が	く	せ	い	で	す	。	か	の
no	ri	ko	sa	n	wa	ryu		u	ga	ku	se	i	de	su		ka	no

じ	ょ	は	に	ほ	ん	か	ら	き	ま	し	た	。
jo		wa	ni	ho	n	ka	ra	ki	ma	shi	ta	

➡ Now try CD L4 part 9.

れんしゅう　1

なまえ（　　　　　　　　　　）

Fill the box with the corresponding hiragana.

a	i	u	e	o
ka	ki	ku	ke	ko
sa	shi	su	se	so
ta	chi	tsu	te	to
na	ni	nu	ne	no
ha	hi	fu	he	ho
ma	mi	mu	me	mo
ya		yu		yo
ra	ri	ru	re	ro
wa				wo
n				

ga	gi	gu	ge	go
za	ji	zu	ze	zo
da	ji	du	de	do
ba	bi	bu	be	bo
pa	pi	pu	pe	po

kya	kyu	kyo
gya	gyu	gyo
sha	shu	sho
ja	ju	jo
cha	chu	cho
nya	nyu	nyo
hya	hyu	hyo
bya	byu	byo
mya	myu	myo
rya	ryu	ryo
pya	pyu	pyo

れんしゅう　2

なまえ（　　　　　　　　）

Draw a line connecting the matching pairs. （あ～ん、voiced sound）

(1)

き	う	け	か	お	い	こ	く	あ	え
ko	a	ka	e	ki	o	i	ku	ke	u

(2)

つ	さ	と	し	て	そ	す	ち	た	せ
sa	tsu	su	chi	shi	to	ta	te	se	so

(3)

ぬ	ね	ほ	は	に	な	ふ	ひ	へ	の
ha	na	hi	no	ne	he	nu	ni	ho	fu

(4)

ゆ	む	も	め	よ	ま	や	み
yu	ma	mi	ya	mu	mo	me	yo

(5)

わ	れ	ん	る	を	ろ	ら	り
•	•	•	•	•	•	•	•
•	•	•	•	•	•	•	•
ro	ri	re	wo	ra	n	wa	ru

(6)

ぎ	ぞ	が	げ	ず	ざ	じ	ご	ぜ	ぐ
•	•	•	•	•	•	•	•	•	•
•	•	•	•	•	•	•	•	•	•
za	ge	ze	gu	go	ji	gi	zo	ga	zu

(7)

ぶ	び	づ	ぼ	ぢ	で	だ	ば	べ	ど
•	•	•	•	•	•	•	•	•	•
•	•	•	•	•	•	•	•	•	•
ji	zu	bo	bu	de	da	be	bi	do	ba

(8)

ぽ	ぱ	ぷ	ぺ	ぴ
•	•	•	•	•
•	•	•	•	•
pa	pu	pi	po	pe

Draw a line connecting matching pairs. （Y-sound）

(9)

しょ	きゃ	しゃ	ちゅ	きゅ	しゅ	きょ	ちょ	ちゃ
•	•	•	•	•	•	•	•	•
•	•	•	•	•	•	•	•	•
kya	shu	chu	cho	kyo	cha	sha	sho	kyu

(10)

みょ	ひゅ	みゃ	にょ	ひゃ	にゅ	ひょ	にゃ	みゅ
•	•	•	•	•	•	•	•	•
•	•	•	•	•	•	•	•	•
hya	nyo	myu	mya	hyu	nyu	myo	nya	hyo

(11)

じょ	じゃ	じゅ	ぎゅ	りゅ	ぎゃ	りょ	ぎょ	りゃ
•	•	•	•	•	•	•	•	•
•	•	•	•	•	•	•	•	•
gya	ju	ryo	ryu	ja	rya	jo	gyo	gyu

(12)

びゃ	ぴゅ	ぴょ	びょ	びゅ	ぴゃ
•	•	•	•	•	•
•	•	•	•	•	•
pya	byu	byo	pyu	bya	pyo

れんしゅう 3

なまえ（　　　　　　）

1. Write in hiragana. （あ～そ）

so (　　) e (　　) ka (　　)
shi (　　) ke (　　) sa (　　)
ki (　　) i (　　) su (　　)
se (　　) ko (　　) u (　　)
a (　　) ku (　　) o (　　)

2. Write in hiragana. （た～ほ）

na (　　) chi (　　) ni (　　)
hi (　　) tsu (　　) ha (　　)
he (　　) ne (　　) ta (　　)
no (　　) te (　　) nu (　　)
fu (　　) ho (　　) to (　　)

3. Write in hiragana. （ま～ん）

n (　　) re (　　) mi (　　)
yu (　　) mu (　　) ya (　　)
me (　　) ri (　　) wa (　　)
ra (　　) wo (　　) yo (　　)
mo (　　) ro (　　) ru (　　)
ma (　　)

れんしゅう 4

なまえ (   )

Write the words in hiragana inside the ( ) and choose the corresponding English word in the [ ].

1. あ to そ

(1) e ( ) [ ]   (2) ie ( ) [ ]

(3) aoi ( ) [ ]   (4) akai ( ) [ ]

(5) ki ( ) [ ]   (6) eki ( ) [ ]

(7) isu ( ) [ ]   (8) kasa ( ) [ ]

(a) station (b) umbrella (c) house (d) blue (e) red (f) painting (g) tree (h) chair

2. た to ほ

(1) inu ( ) [ ]   (2) tsukue ( ) [ ]

(3) hito ( ) [ ]   (4) takai ( ) [ ]

(5) neko ( ) [ ]   (6) shita ( ) [ ]

(7) fune ( ) [ ]   (8) hako ( ) [ ]

(a) box (b) expensive (c) desk (d) ship (e) cat (f) dog (g) person (h) below

3. ま to ん

(1) umi ( ) [ ]   (2) namae ( ) [ ]

(3) yama ( ) [ ]   (4) nihon ( ) [ ]

(5) hare ( ) [ ]   (6) kusuri ( ) [ ]

(7) ame ( ) [ ]   (8) watashi ( ) [ ]

(a) ocean (b) Japan (c) name (d) mountain (e) clear sky (f) I (g) medicine (h) rain

4. が〜、ざ〜、だ〜

(1) nihongo ( ) [ ]　(2) kagi ( ) [ ]

(3) ongaku ( ) [ ]　(4) denwa ( ) [ ]

(5) daigaku ( ) [ ]　(6) gozen ( ) [ ]

(7) kazoku ( ) [ ]　(8) doko ( ) [ ]

(a) family (b) the Japanese language (c) university (d) telephone (e) key (f) where (g) AM (h) music

5. ば〜、ぱ〜

(1) kanpai ( ) [ ]　(2) ebi ( ) [ ]

(3) tabemasu ( ) [ ]　(4) enpitsu ( ) [ ]

(5) shinbun ( ) [ ]　(6) kaban ( ) [ ]

(a) bag (b) to eat (c) shrimp (d) pencil (e) toast (f) newspaper

6. Stop Sound & Long Vowels

Note that the roma-ji for a long vowel refers to the pronunciation, not the spelling.

(1) kippu ( ) [ ]　(2) kitte ( ) [ ]

(3) zasshi ( ) [ ]　(4) eego ( ) [ ]

(5) otoosan ( ) [ ]　(6) tokee ( ) [ ]

(7) gakusee ( ) [ ]　(8) ookii ( ) [ ]

(9) okaasan ( ) [ ]　(10) tooi ( ) [ ]

(a) far (b) English (c) stamp (d) mother (e) big (f) student (g) father (h) magazine (i) ticket (j) watch

8. きゃ〜、ぎゃ〜、しゃ〜、じゃ〜、ちゃ〜

(1) kyookai ( ) [ ] (2) gyuunyuu ( ) [ ]

(3) kaisha ( ) [ ] (4) shukudai ( ) [ ]

(5) ocha ( ) [ ] (6) kyookasho ( ) [ ]

(7) chotto ( ) [ ] (8) jyuudoo ( ) [ ]

(a) textbook (b) milk (c) church (d) homework (e) company (f) Judo (g) a bit (h) tea

9. にゃ〜、ひゃ〜、びゃ〜、ぴゃ〜、みゃ〜、りゃ〜

(1) hyaku ( ) [ ] (2) roppyaku ( ) [ ]

(3) byooin ( ) [ ] (4) ryuugaku ( ) [ ]

(5) myooji ( ) [ ] (6) gyuunyuu ( ) [ ]

(7) ryokoo ( ) [ ] (8) sanbyaku ( ) [ ]

(a) hospital (b) trip (c) three hundreds (d) study abroad (e) hundred (f) milk (g) six hundreds (h) last name

れんしゅう 5

なまえ（　　　　　　　　）

Look at the pictures and write their names in hiragana.

(1)

house

(2)
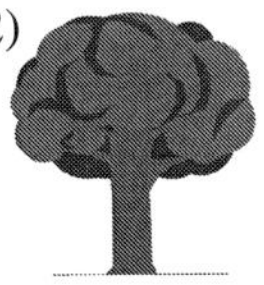
tree

(3)

umbrella

(4)

chair

(5)

desk

(6)
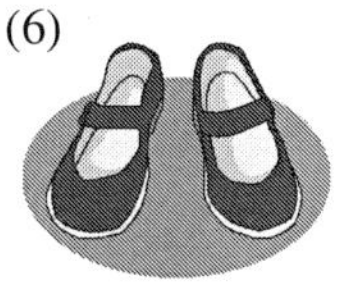
shoes

(7)

dog

(8)

ship

(9)

rain

(10)

mountain

(11)

clear sky

(12)

book

(13)
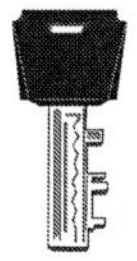
key

(14)

telephone

(15)

bag

(16)
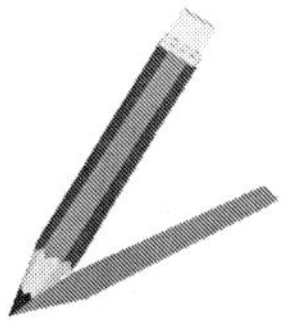
(wooden) pencil

(17)

(transportation) ticket

(18)

stamp

(19)

clock/watch

(20)

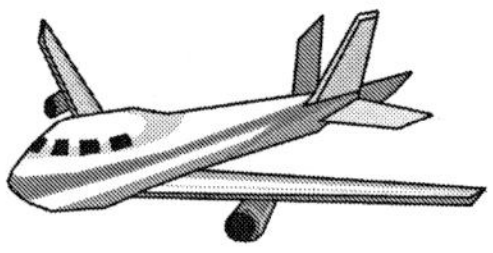

airplane

(21)

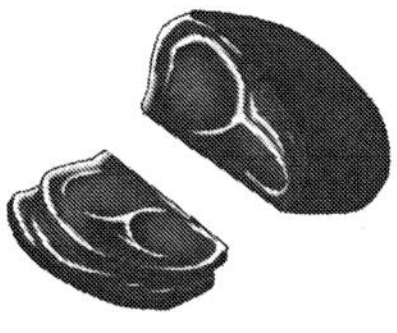

meat

(22)

sweets/snack

(23)

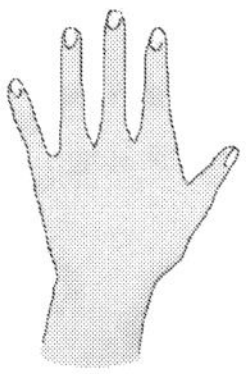

hand

(24)

to write

(25)

snow

(26)

to read

(27)

cherry blossom

(28)

Japan

(29)

newspaper

(30)

toast

(31)

musical instruments

(32)

milk

(33)

church

(34)

beef

Now try CD Lesson 5.

れんしゅう　6：Numbers

なまえ（　　　　　　　　）

Let's write numbers.

1

i	chi

2

ni

3

sa	n

4

yo	n

(4)

shi

5

go

6

ro	ku

7

na	na

(7)

shi	chi

8

ha	chi

9

kyu		u

(9)

ku

10

ju		u

Let's write months.

January

i	chi	ga	tsu

February

ni	ga	tsu

March

sa	n	ga	tsu

April

shi	ga	tsu

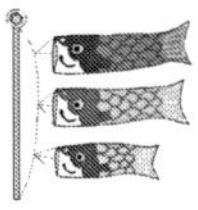

May

go	ga	tsu

June

ro	ku	ga	tsu

July

shi	chi	ga	tsu

August

ha	chi	ga	tsu

September

ku	ga	tsu

October

ju		u	ga	tsu

November

ju		u	i	chi	ga	tsu

December

ju		u	ni	ga	tsu

れんしゅう　7：Family

なまえ（　　　　　　　　）

My Family: Fill in the box using hiragana. Note that the roma-ji beneath the box for a long vowel refers to the pronunciation, not the spelling.

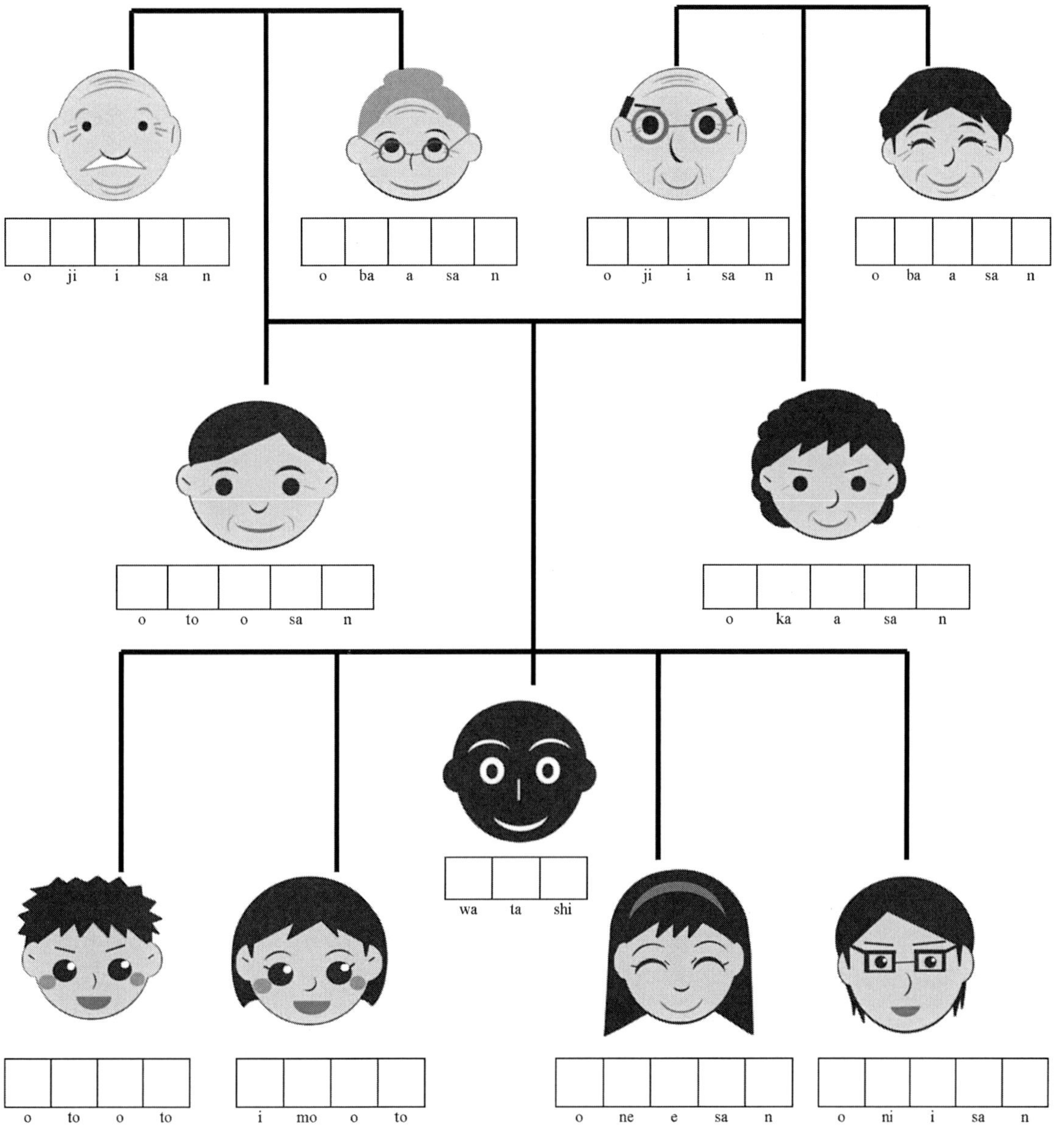

Now try CD Lesson 6.

れんしゅう 8：Body

なまえ（ ）

Fill in the box using hiragana.

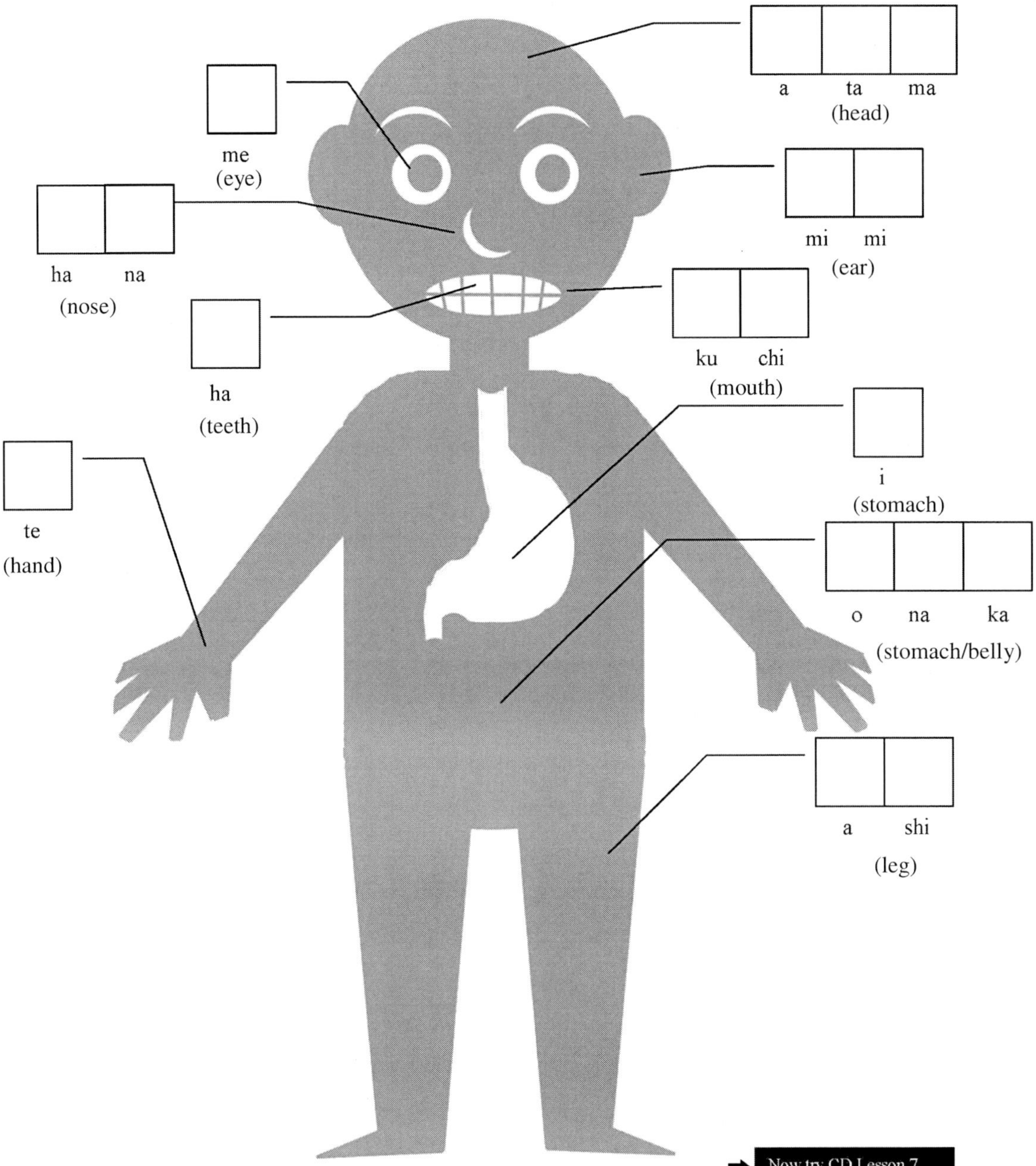

Now try CD Lesson 7.

れんしゅう　9：Classroom　　　なまえ（　　　　　　　　）

Fill in the box using hiragana. Note that the roma-ji beneath the box for a long vowel refers to the pronunciation, not the spelling.

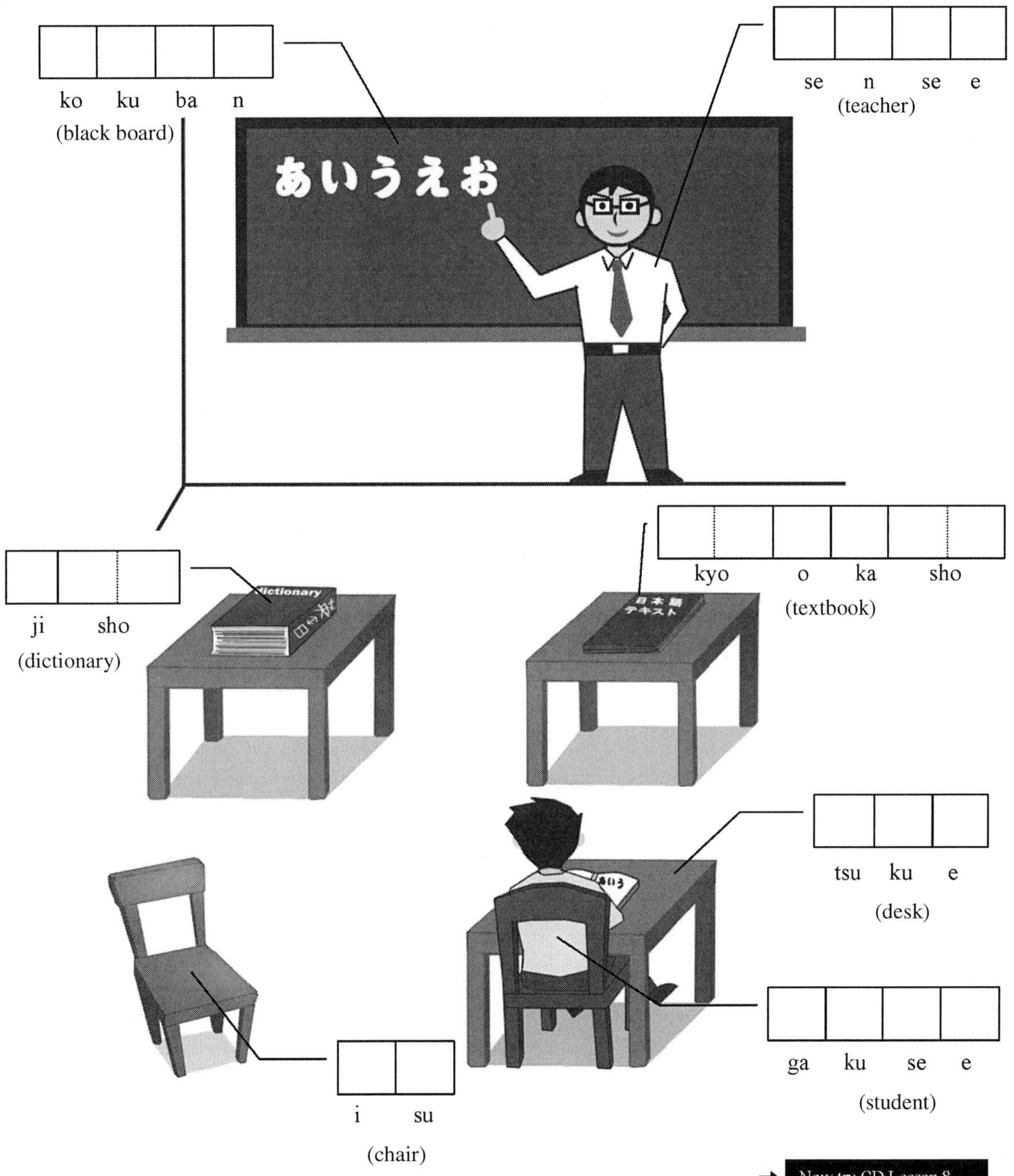

Now try CD Lesson 8.

Part Two:

Katakana Practice カタカナ れんしゅう

BASIC SOUNDS ♪♫

	a	i	u	e	o
	ア a	イ i	ウ u	エ e	オ o
k	カ ka	キ ki	ク ku	ケ ke	コ ko
s	サ sa	シ **shi**	ス su	セ se	ソ so
t	タ ta	チ **chi**	ツ **tsu**	テ te	ト to
n	ナ na	ニ ni	ヌ nu	ネ ne	ノ no
h	ハ ha	ヒ hi	フ fu	ヘ he	ホ ho
m	マ ma	ミ mi	ム mu	メ me	モ mo
y	ヤ ya	(イ)	ユ yu	(エ)	ヨ yo
r	ラ ra	リ ri	ル ru	レ re	ロ ro
w	ワ wa	(イ)	(ウ)	(エ)	ヲ wo (=o)
N	ン n				

VOICED SOUNDS AND Y-SOUNDS

	a	i	u	e	o
g	ガ ga	ギ gi	グ gu	ゲ ge	ゴ go
z	ザ za	ジ ji	ズ zu	ゼ ze	ゾ zo
d	ダ da	ヂ ji	ヅ zu	デ de	ド do
b	バ ba	ビ bi	ブ bu	ベ be	ボ bo
p	パ pa	ピ pi	プ pu	ペ pe	ポ po

Y-SOUNDS

	a	u	o
ky	キャ kya	キュ kyu	キョ kyo
gy	ギャ gya	ギュ gyu	ギョ gyo
sh	シャ sha	シュ shu	ショ sho
j	ジャ ja	ジュ ju	ジョ jo
ch	チャ cha	チュ chu	チョ cho
ny	ニャ nya	ニュ nyu	ニョ nyo
hy	ヒャ hya	ヒュ hyu	ヒョ hyo
by	ビャ bya	ビュ byu	ビョ byo
my	ミャ mya	ミュ myu	ミョ myo
ry	リャ rya	リュ ryu	リョ ryo
py	ピャ pya	ピュ pyu	ピョ pyo

FOREIGN SOUNDS

	a	i	u	e	o
i				イェ yie	
u		ウィ wui		ウェ wue	ウォ wuo
ku	クァ kua	クィ kui		クェ kue	クォ kuo
gu	グァ gua	グィ gui		グェ gue	グォ guo
shi				シェ she	
ji				ジェ je	
chi				チェ che	
tsu	ツァ tsua	ツィ tsui		ツェ tsue	ツォ tsuo
te		ティ ti	テュ tyu		
de		ディ di	デュ dyu		
to			トゥ tu		
do			ドゥ du		
fu	ファ hua	フィ hui	フュ hyu	フェ hue	フォ huo
vu			ヴ vu		
vu	ヴァ va	ヴィ vi	ヴュ vyu	ヴェ vue	ヴォ vuo

Listen to CD Lesson 1 for the sounds and see the stroke order.

PRACTICE WRITING

What is wrong?

a* to *o

ア	a	ア	ア	ア			
イ	i	イ	イ	イ			
ウ	u	ウ	ウ	ウ			
エ	e	エ	エ	エ			
オ	o	オ	オ	オ			

KNOWLEDGE:

Hiragana has a roundish shape, but katakana has rather straight lines. Compare the difference.

う vs. ウ

Hiragana is developed from the cursive of kanji. Original kanji of hiragana are:

安→あ　以→い　宇→う　衣→え　於→お

On the other hand, katakana took a part of kanji.

阿→ア　伊→イ　宇→ウ　江→エ　於→オ

ka* to *ko

カ	ka	カ	カ	カ			
キ	ki	キ	キ	キ			
ク	ku	ク	ク	ク			
ケ	ke	ケ	ケ	ケ			
コ	ko	コ	コ	コ			

How are they different?

カ & か

キ & き

ク & ワ

ケ & ク

Let's read and write! Guess what these words mean in English!

ココア

コ	コ	ア

キウイ

キ	ウ	イ

カカオ

カ	カ	オ

Let's write a sentence.

In the first sentence below, のみます (*nomimasu*) is 'to drink'. In the second sentence, たべます (*tabemasu*) is 'to eat'.

1) (I) drink cocoa.

コ	コ	ア	を	の	み	ま	す	。
ko	ko	a	wo	no	mi	ma	su	

2) (I) eat a kiwi.

キ	ウ	イ	を	た	べ	ま	す	。
ki	u	i	wo	ta	be	ma	su	

Now try CD L2 part 1 & L3 part 1.

sa* to *so

サ	sa	①②③ サ	サ	サ				
シ	shi	①②③ シ	シ	シ				
ス	su	①② ス	ス	ス				
セ	se	①② セ	セ	セ				
ソ	so	①② ソ	ソ	ソ				

How are they different?

シ & ツ

ス & ヌ

セ & せ

ソ & ン

Let's read and write.

アイス

ア	イ	ス

スイス

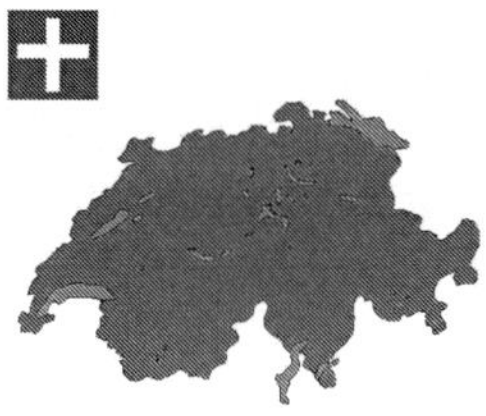

ス	イ	ス

キス

キ	ス

Let's write a sentence.

1) (I) eat ice cream.

ア	イ	ス	を	た	べ	ま	す	。
a	i	su	wo	ta	be	ma	su	

➡ Now try CD L4 part

ta* to *to

タ	ta	タ	タ	タ				
チ	chi	チ	チ	チ				
ツ	tsu	ツ	ツ	ツ				
テ	te	テ	テ	テ				
ト	to	ト	ト	ト				

How are they different?

タ & ク

チ & 千

ツ & シ

What is wrong?

ト ←

Let's read and write.

ウエスト

ウエスト

ツイスト

ツイスト

テスト

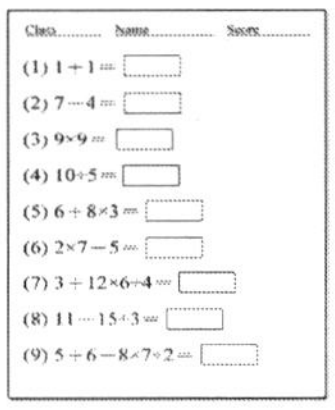

テスト

Let's write a sentence.
In the sentence below, おどります (*odorimasu*) is 'to dance'.

1) (I) dance the twist.

ツ	イ	ス	ト	を	お	ど	り	ま	す	。
tsu	i	su	to	wo	o	do	ri	ma	su	

➡ Now try CD L2 part 2 & L3 part 2.

na to *no*

ナ	na	①→ ②↓ ナ	ナ	ナ				
ニ	ni	①→ ②→ ニ	ニ	ニ				
ヌ	nu	① ② ヌ	ヌ	ヌ				
ネ	ne	① ② ③ ④ ネ	ネ	ネ				
ノ	no	① ノ	ノ	ノ				

What is wrong?

Let's read and write.

テニス

テ	ニ	ス

ケニア

ケ	ニ	ア

ネクタイ

ネ	ク	タ	イ

Let's write a sentence.

In the first sentence below, します (*shimasu*) is 'to do' or 'to play (sports)'. In the second sentence, します (*shimasu*) means 'to put on'.

1) (I) play tennis.

テ	ニ	ス	を	し	ま	す	。
te	ni	su	wo	shi	ma	su	

2) (I) put on a necktie.

ネ	ク	タ	イ	を	し	ま	す	。
ne	ku	ta	i	wo	shi	ma	su	

What is wrong?

ha* to *ho

ハ	ha	ハ	ハ	ハ			
ヒ	hi	ヒ	ヒ	ヒ			
フ	fu	フ	フ	フ			
ヘ	he	ヘ	ヘ	ヘ			
ホ	ho	ホ	ホ	ホ			

Let's read and write.

ハイテク

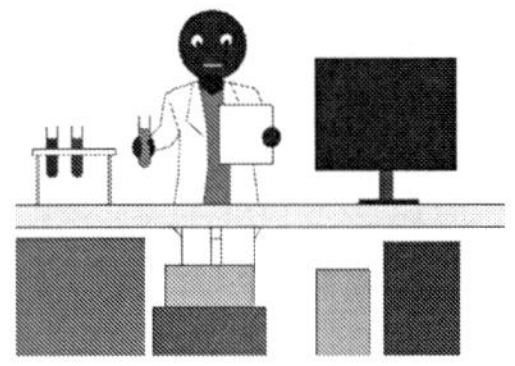

ハ	イ	テ	ク

ハノイ

ハ	ノ	イ

ナイフ

ナ	イ	フ

Let's write a sentence.

In the sentence below, いきます (*ikimasu*) is 'to go'. You need the particle に (*ni*) after a destination. In this case ハノイ 'Hanoi' is a destination.

1) (I will) go to Hanoi.

ハ	ノ	イ	に	い	き	ま	す	。
ha	no	i	ni	i	ki	ma	su	

➡ Now try CD L2 part 3 & L3 part 3.
After that try L4 part 2

ma* to *mo

マ	ma	マ	マ	マ				
ミ	mi	ミ	ミ	ミ				
ム	mu	ム	ム	ム				
メ	me	メ	メ	メ				
モ	mo	モ	モ	モ				

What is wrong?

Let's read and write.

トマト

ト	マ	ト

マイナス

45−18=27

マ	イ	ナ	ス

メモ

メ	モ

Let's write a sentence.

1) (I) eat tomatoes.

ト	マ	ト	を	た	べ	ま	す	。
to	ma	to	wo	ta	be	ma	su	

ya* to *yo

ヤ	ya	ヤ	ヤ	ヤ				
ユ	yu	ユ	ユ	ユ				
ヨ	yo	ヨ	ヨ	ヨ				

How are they different?

や & ヤ

ユ & コ

Let's read and write.

タイヤ

タ	イ	ヤ

ユニセフ

ユ	ニ	セ	フ

ヨセミテ

ヨ	セ	ミ	テ

Let's write a sentence.

1) (I will) go to Yosemite.

ヨ	セ	ミ	テ	に	い	き	ま	す	。
yo	se	mi	te	ni	i	ki	ma	su	

Now try CD L2 part 4 & L3 part 4.

ra* to *ro

ラ	ra	①→ ②→ ラ	ラ	ラ				
リ	ri	①↓ ②↓ リ	リ	リ				
ル	ru	①↓ ②↓ ル	ル	ル				
レ	re	①↓ レ	レ	レ				
ロ	ro	①↓ ②→ ③→ ロ	ロ	ロ				

How are they different?

ラ & フ

リ & り

ル & ハ

Let's read and write.

クラス

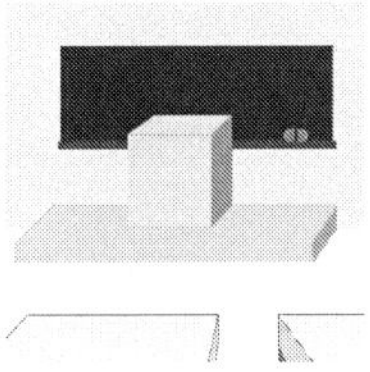

ク	ラ	ス

カメラ

カ	メ	ラ

アメリカ

ア	メ	リ	カ

ホテル

ホ	テ	ル

トイレ

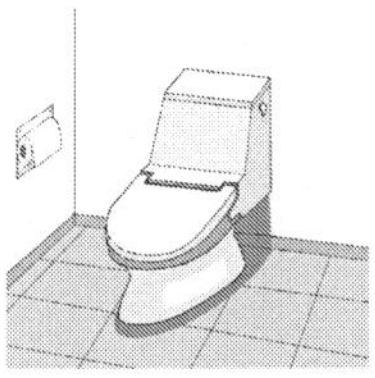

ト	イ	レ

カラオケ

カ	ラ	オ	ケ

Let's write a sentence.

In the sentence below, かいます (*kaimasu*) is 'to buy'.

1) (I will) buy a camera.

カ	メ	ラ	を	か	い	ま	す	。
ka	me	ra	wo	ka	i	ma	su	

➡ Now try CD L4 part 3.

wa & wo

ワ	wa	①②ワ	ワ	ワ				
ヲ	wo	①②ヲ	ヲ	ヲ				

How are they different?

ワ & ク

ヲ & フ

Let's read and write.

ワイヤレス

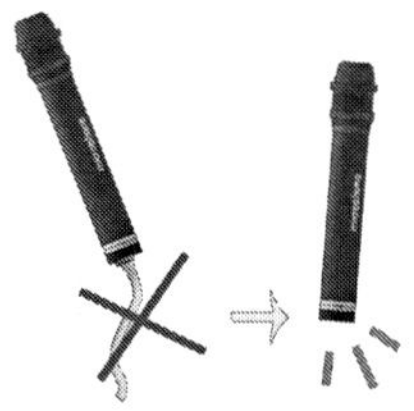

ワ	イ	ヤ	レ	ス

ホワイトハウス

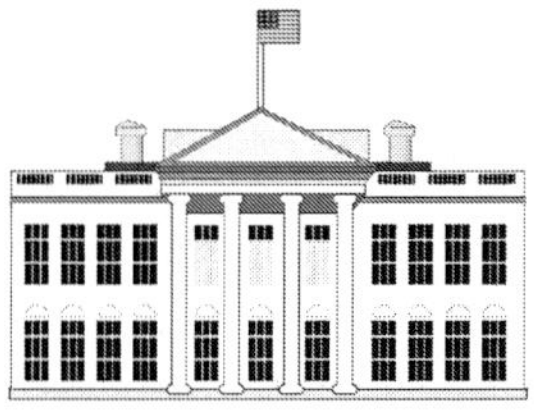

ホ	ワ	イ	ト	ハ	ウ	ス

Let's write a sentence.

In the sentence below, おおきい (*ookii*) is 'big'.

1) The White House is big.

ホ	ワ	イ	ト	ハ	ウ	ス	は	お	お	き	い	で	す	。
ho	wa	i	to	ha	u	su	wa	o	o	ki	i	de	su	

How are they different?

n

ン	n	①② ン	ン	ン				

ン & ソ

Let's read and write.

ワイン

ワ	イ	ン

レモン

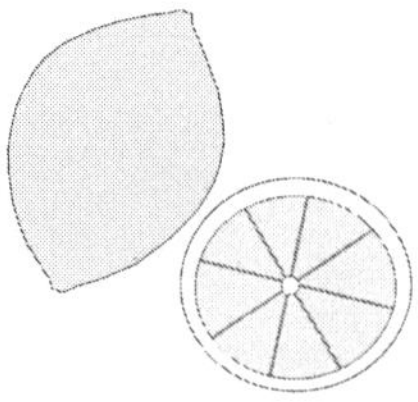

レ	モ	ン

ハンサム

ハ	ン	サ	ム

レストラン

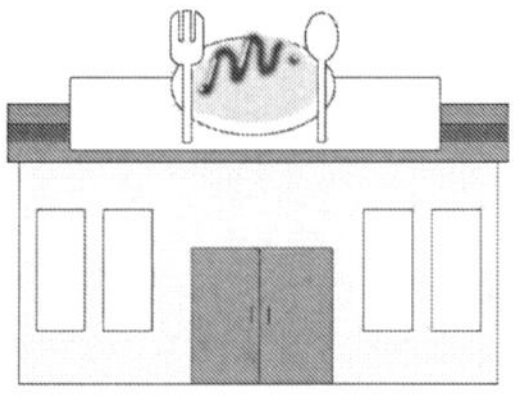

レ	ス	ト	ラ	ン

エアコン

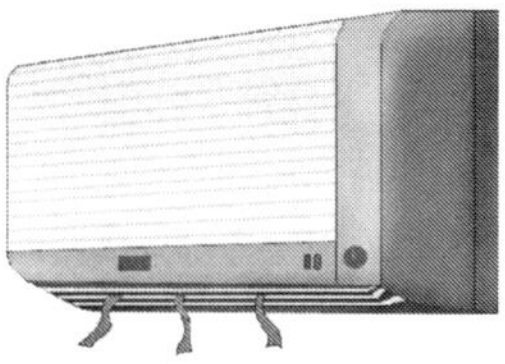

エ	ア	コ	ン

ランチ

ラ	ン	チ

Let's write a sentence.

In the sentence below, そして (*soshite*) means 'and' which connects two sentences. Let's put a comma after そして. Please notice that the Japanese comma is down and to the right.

1) (I) eat lunch. And (I) drink wine.

ラ	ン	チ	を	た	べ	ま	す	。	そ	し	て	、	ワ	イ	ン	を
ra	n	chi	wo	ta	be	ma	su		so	shi	te		wa	i	n	wo

の	み	ま	す	。
no	mi	ma	su	

Now try CD L2 part 5 & L3 part 5.
After that try L4 part 4.

VOICED SOUNDS AND P-SOUNDS

Voiced sounds are indicated by basic katakana with '*tenten*' (two short lines on top).

ga* to *go

ガ	ギ	グ	ゲ	ゴ
ga	gi	gu	ge	go

Let's read and write.

ヨガ

ヨ	ガ

イギリス

イ	ギ	リ	ス

カタログ

カ	タ	ロ	グ

ゲスト

ゲ	ス	ト

レントゲン

レ	ン	ト	ゲ	ン

ゴルフ

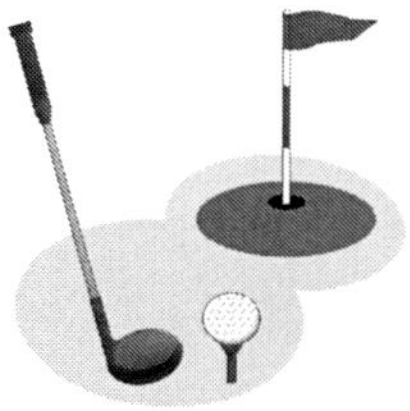

ゴ	ル	フ

Let's write a sentence.

In the sentence below, みます (*mimasu*) means 'to look at' or 'to watch'.

1) (I) look at catalogues.

カ	タ	ロ	グ	を	み	ま	す	。
ka	ta	ro	gu	wo	mi	ma	su	

za* to *zo

ザ	ジ	ズ	ゼ	ゾ
za	ji	zu	ze	zo

Let's read and write.

ラジオ

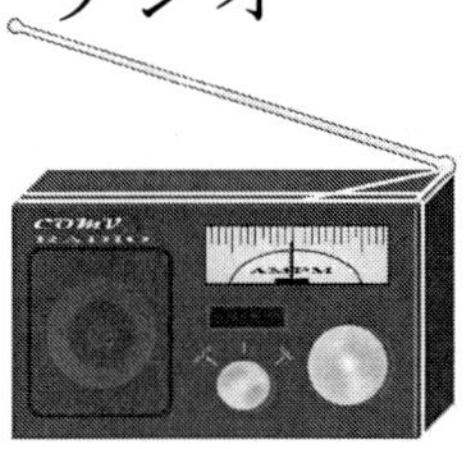

ラ	ジ	オ

サイズ

サ	イ	ズ

ゼロ

ゼ	ロ

Let's write a sentence.

In the sentence below, ききます (*kikimasu*) is 'to listen'.

1) (I) listen to the radio.

ラ	ジ	オ	を	き	き	ま	す	。
ra	ji	o	wo	ki	ki	ma	su	

da to *do*

ダ	ヂ	ヅ	デ	ド
da	ji	zu	de	do

Note: There are no words that use katakana ヂ or ヅ.

Let's read and write.

ダンス

マクドナルド

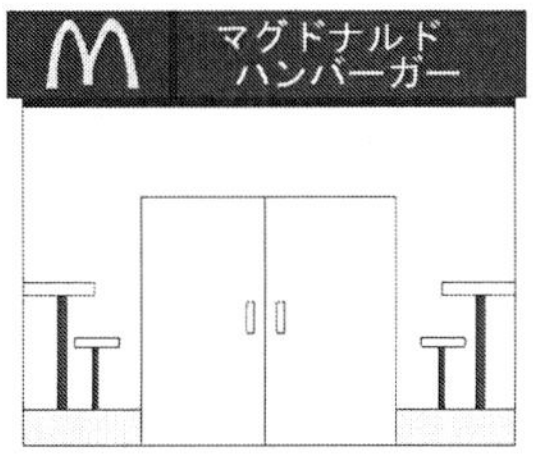

ドア

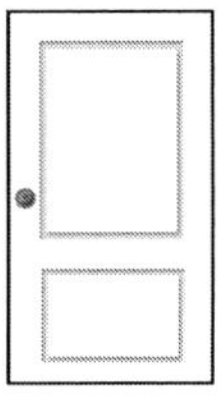

ダ	ン	ス

マ	ク	ド	ナ	ル	ド

ド	ア

Let's write a sentence.

1) (I) watch dramas.

ド	ラ	マ	を	み	ま	す	。
do	ra	ma	wo	mi	ma	su	

➡ Now try CD L4 part 5.

ba* to *bo

バ	ビ	ブ	ベ	ボ
ba	bi	bu	be	bo

Let's read and write.

バス

バ	ス

タバコ

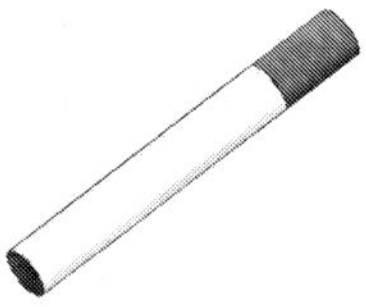

タ	バ	コ

アルバイト

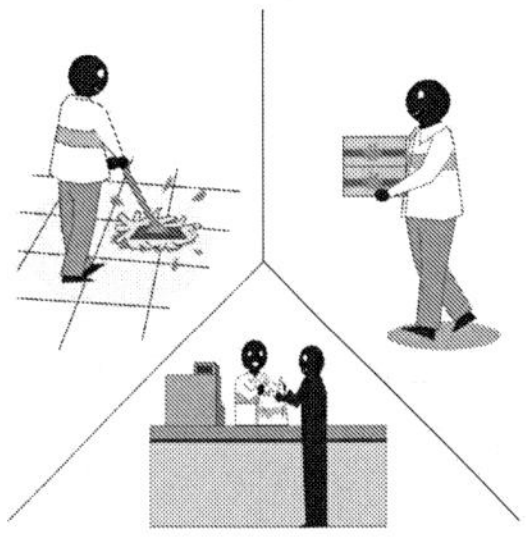

Note: The word 'アルバイト' is originally from Germany. It means 'part-time job'

ア	ル	バ	イ	ト

テレビ

テ	レ	ビ

コンビニ

コ	ン	ビ	ニ

ドライブ

ド	ラ	イ	ブ

Let's write a sentence.

In the sentence below, you need the particle で (*de*) after a place, マクドナルド in this example. で (*de*) corresponds to English 'at' or 'in'. します (*shimasu*) means 'to do'. Be aware that the Japanese language word order is 'Topic-Place-Object-Verb'.

1) I work part-time at Macdonald's.

わ	た	し	は	マ	ク	ド	ナ	ル	ド	で	ア	ル	バ	イ	ト	を
wa	ta	shi	wa	ma	ku	do	na	ru	do	de	a	ru	ba	i	to	wo

し	ま	す	。
shi	ma	su	

pa* to *po

パ	ピ	プ	ペ	ポ
pa	pi	pu	pe	po

Let's read and write.

ピアノ

ピ	ア	ノ

ポスト

ポ	ス	ト

プレゼント

プ	レ	ゼ	ン	ト

パンツ

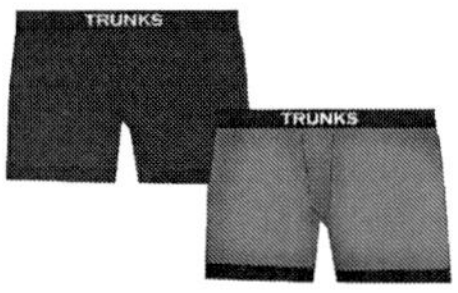

パ	ン	ツ

ペン

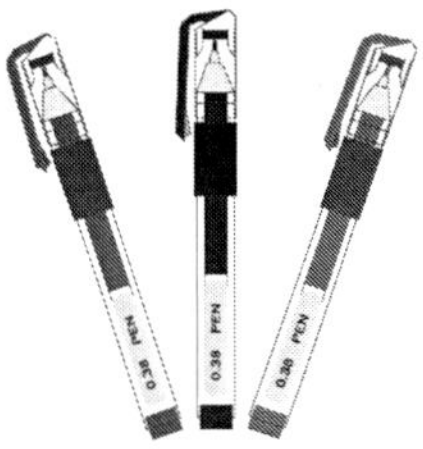

ペ	ン

パン

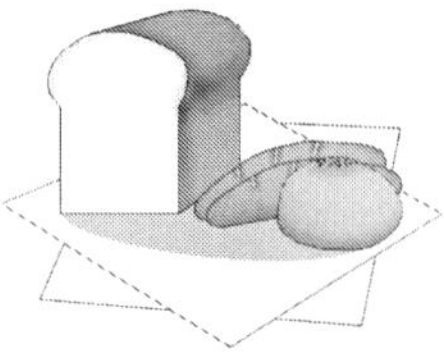

パ	ン

パソコン

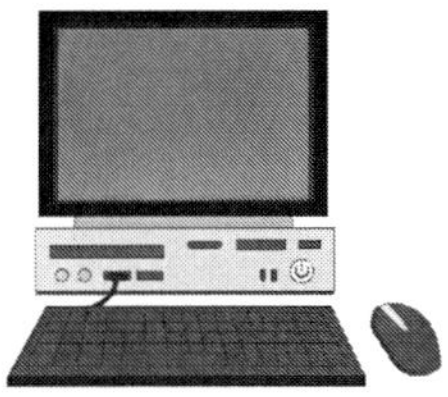

パ	ソ	コ	ン

Let's write a sentence.

In the sentence below, かいます (*kaimasu*) is 'to buy'.

1) (I will) buy a present.

プ	レ	ゼ	ン	ト	を	か	い	ま	す	。
pu	re	ze	n	to	wo	ka	i	ma	su	

Now try CD L4 part 6.

STOPPED SOUNDS

Stopped sounds are indicated by small ‘ッ’ (*tsu*). ‘ッ’ is quarter size.

ッ	

Let’s read and write.

カップ

カ	ッ	プ

コップ

コ	ッ	プ

クラシック

ク	ラ	シ	ッ	ク

チケット

チ	ケ	ッ	ト

ベッド

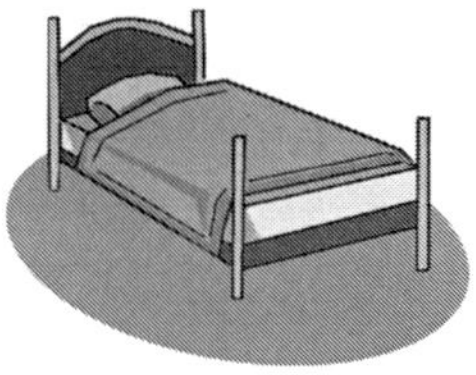

ベ	ッ	ド

ホッチキス

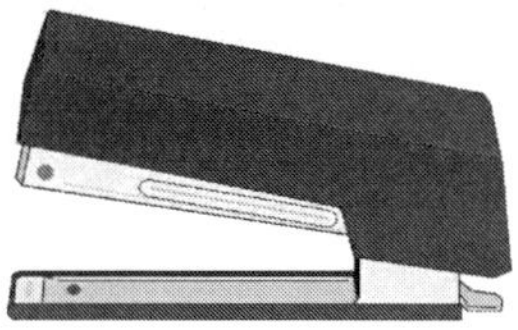

ホ	ッ	チ	キ	ス

Let’s write a sentence.

1) (I) listen to classical (music).

ク	ラ	シ	ッ	ク	を	き	き	ま	す	。
ku	ra	shi	kku		wo	ki	ki	ma	su	

Now try CD L4 part 7.

Long Vowels

Long sounds in katakana are indicated by hyphen.

Let's read and write.

ノート

ノ	ー	ト

コーヒー

コ	ー	ヒ	ー

ハンバーガー

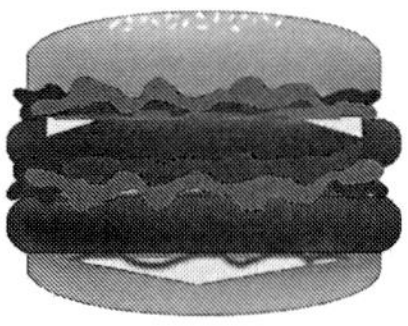

ハ	ン	バ	ー	ガ	ー

テーブル

テ	ー	ブ	ル

ケーキ

ケ	ー	キ

デパート

デ	パ	ー	ト

モール

モ	ー	ル

ウエートレス

ウ	エ	ー	ト	レ	ス

ジーパン

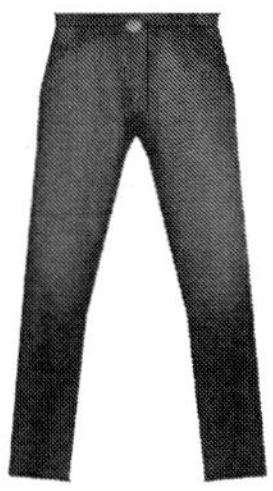

ジ	ー	パ	ン

スポーツ

デート

スーパー

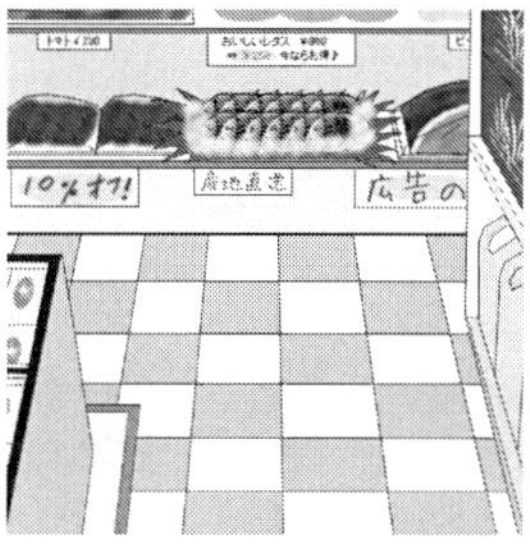

ス	ポ	ー	ツ

デ	ー	ト

ス	ー	パ	ー

アパート

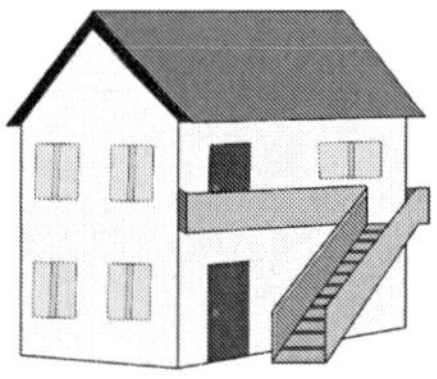

ビール

ルームメート

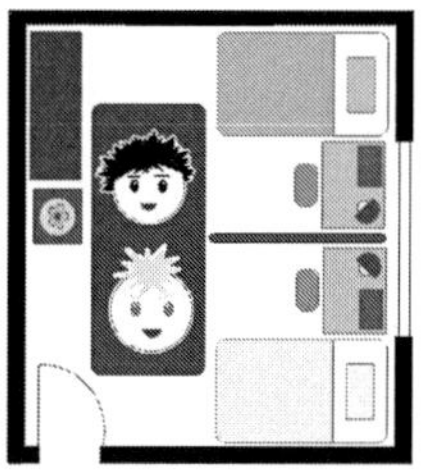

ア	パ	ー	ト

ビ	ー	ル

ル	ー	ム	メ	ー	ト

Let's write a sentence.

Let's write a short composition. In the sentence below, にちようび (*nichiyoobi*) means 'Sunday'. 'To go on a date' in Japanese uses します (*shimasu*) 'to do (a date)'.

1) On Sundays, I go on dates. (I) eat hamburgers at the mall. And (I) buy cakes at the supermarket.

に	ち	よ	う	び	わ	た	し	は	デ	ー	ト	を	し	ま	す	。
ni	chi	yo	o	bi	wa	ta	shi	wa	de	e	to	wo	shi	ma	su	
モ	ー	ル	で	ハ	ン	バ	ー	ガ	ー	を	た	べ	ま	す	。	そ
mo	o	ru	de	ha	n	ba	a	ga	a	wo	ta	be	ma	su		so
し	て	、	ス	ー	パ	ー	で	ケ	ー	キ	を	か	い	ま	す	。
shi	te		su	u	pa	a	de	ke	e	ki	wo	ka	i	ma	su	

➡ Now try CD L4 part 8.

Y-SOUNDS

'ヤ', 'ユ', 'ヨ' are quarter size.

Let's read and write.

キャンプ

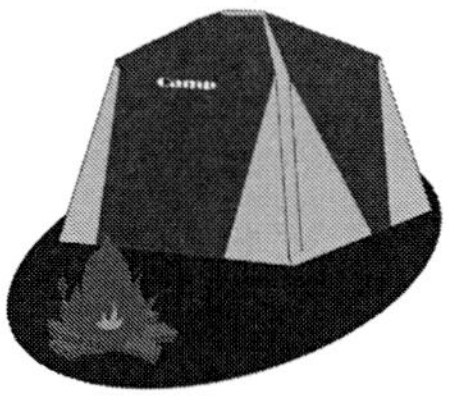

キ	ャ	ン	プ

シャツ

シ	ャ	ツ

シャーペン

シ	ャ	ー	ペ	ン

ジュース

ジ	ュ	ー	ス

ニュース

ニ	ュ	ー	ス

メニュー

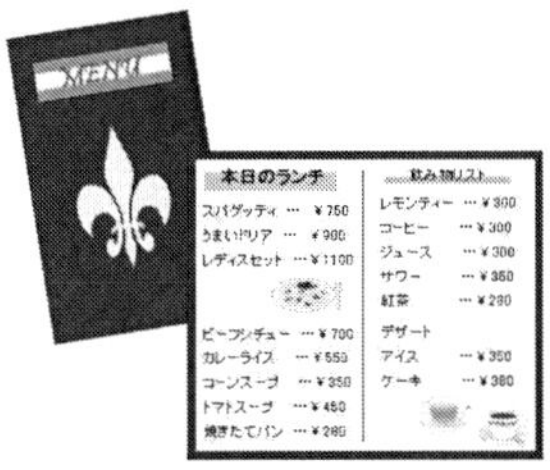

メ	ニ	ュ	ー

コンピュータ

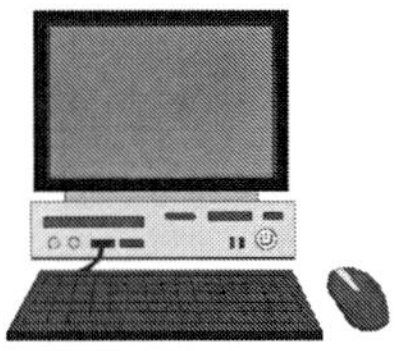

コ	ン	ピ	ュ	ー	タ

バーベキュー

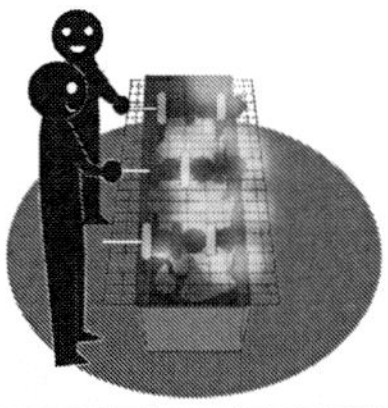

バ	ー	ベ	キ	ュ	ー

チョコレート

チ	ョ	コ	レ	ー	ト

ジョギング

ジ	ョ	ギ	ン	グ

Let's write a small composition.

In the first sentence below, でも (*demo*) means 'but'. Please note that ジョギング *(jogingu)* 'jog' in the first example and バーベキュー (*baabekyuu*) 'barbeque' in the second example use the verb します (*shimasu*) 'to do'.

1) I eat chocolate. But (I) jog.

わ	た	し	は	チ	ョ	コ	レ	ー	ト	を	た	べ	ま	す	。
wa	ta	shi	wa	cho	ko		re	e	to	wo	ta	be	ma	su	
で	も	、	ジ	ョ	ギ	ン	グ	を	し	ま	す	。			
de	mo		jo		gi	n	gu	wo	shi	ma	su				

2) I barbeque at the camp (site).

わ	た	し	は	キ	ャ	ン	プ	で	バ	ー	ベ	キ	ュ	ー	を
wa	ta	shi	wa	kya		n	pu	de	ba	a	be	kyu		u	wo
し	ま	す	。												
shi	ma	su													

Now try CD L4 part 9.

OTHERS

Let's read and write.

スパゲッティ

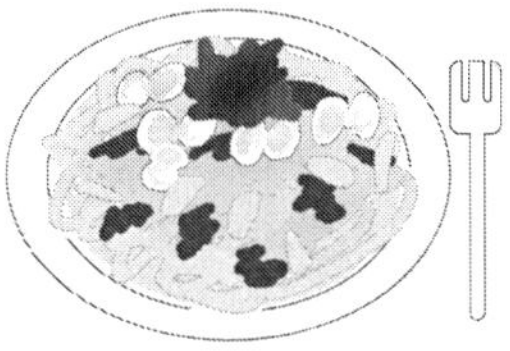

ス	パ	ゲ	ッ	テ	ィ

パーティー

パ	ー	テ	ィ	ー

ティーシャツ

テ	ィ	ー	シ	ャ	ツ

レモンティー

レ	モ	ン	テ	ィ	ー

キャンディー

キ	ャ	ン	デ	ィ	ー

ウェディング

ウ	ェ	デ	ィ	ン	グ

ウィスキー

ウ	ィ	ス	キ	ー

シェーキ

シ	ェ	ー	キ

ソファー

ソ	フ	ァ	ー

フォーク

フ	ォ	ー	ク

ヴァイオリン

ヴ	ァ	イ	オ	リ	ン

フィルム

フ	ィ	ル	ム

テレフォンカード

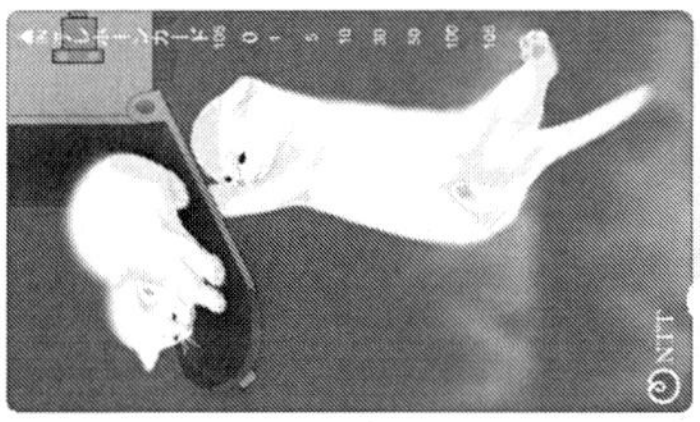

テ	レ	フ	ォ	ン	カ	ー	ド

ファックス

フ	ァ	ッ	ク	ス

ホストファミリー

ホ	ス	ト	フ	ァ	ミ	リ	ー

Let's write a composition.
In the sentence below, きょう (*kyoo*) means 'today'.

1) Today I (will) eat spaghetti. And (I will) drink a shake.

き	ょ	う	わ	た	し	は	ス	パ	ゲ	ッ	テ	ィ	を	た	べ	ま
kyo		o	wa	ta	shi	wa	su	pa	ge		tti		wo	ta	be	ma

す	。	そ	し	て	、	シ	ェ	ー	キ	を	の	み	ま	す	。
su		so	shi	te		she		e	ki	wo	no	mi	ma	su	

Now try CD L5 part 1 to part 5.

れんしゅう 1

なまえ（　　　　　　　）

Fill the box with the corresponding katakana.

a	i	u	e	o
ka	ki	ku	ke	ko
sa	shi	su	se	so
ta	chi	tsu	te	to
na	ni	nu	ne	no
ha	hi	fu	he	ho
ma	mi	mu	me	mo
ya		yu		yo
ra	ri	ru	re	ro
wa				wo
n				

ga	gi	gu	ge	go
za	ji	zu	ze	zo
da	ji	du	de	do
ba	bi	bu	be	bo
pa	pi	pu	pe	po

kya	kyu	kyo
gya	gyu	gyo
sha	shu	sho
ja	ju	jo
cha	chu	cho
nya	nyu	nyo
hya	hyu	hyo
bya	byu	byo
mya	myu	myo
rya	ryu	ryo
pya	pyu	pyo

れんしゅう　2

なまえ（　　　　　　　　　　　）

Draw a line connecting the matching pairs.　（ア～ン、voiced sound）

(1)

オ	ケ	ウ	コ	キ	ク	カ	イ	エ	ア
ko	a	ka	e	ki	o	i	ku	ke	u

(2)

サ	ツ	テ	チ	セ	ソ	ス	シ	タ	ト
sa	tsu	su	chi	shi	to	ta	te	se	so

(3)

ホ	ハ	ヌ	ネ	ノ	ヒ	フ	ナ	ヘ	ニ
ha	na	hi	no	ne	he	nu	ni	ho	fu

(4)

ヤ	ム	モ	マ	ミ	メ	ユ	ヨ
yu	ma	mi	ya	mu	mo	me	yo

(5)

ン	ロ	ワ	ル	レ	リ	ラ
ro	ri	re	ra	n	wa	ru

(6)

グ	ゲ	ゴ	ゾ	ザ	ズ	ジ	ガ	ゼ	ギ
•	•	•	•	•	•	•	•	•	•
•	•	•	•	•	•	•	•	•	•
za	ge	ze	gu	go	ji	gi	zo	ga	zu

(7)

ビ	ブ	ボ	デ	バ	ダ	ド	ベ
•	•	•	•	•	•	•	•
•	•	•	•	•	•	•	•
ba	de	bo	bu	da	be	bi	do

(8)

プ	パ	ポ	ペ	ピ
•	•	•	•	•
•	•	•	•	•
pa	pu	pi	po	pe

れんしゅう　3

なまえ（　　　　　　　　　　　　）

Circle the character that does not belong.

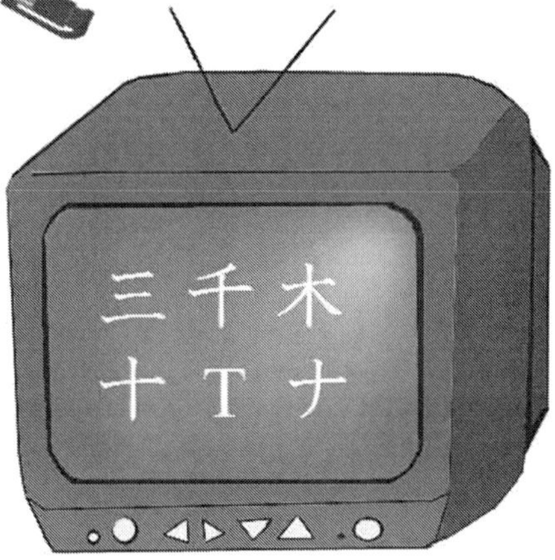

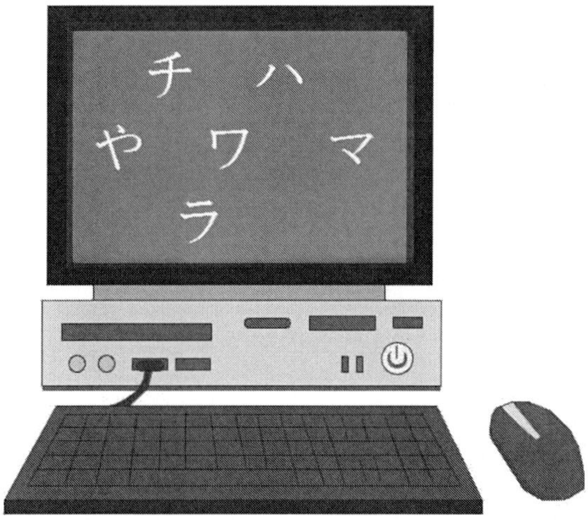

れんしゅう 4

なまえ（ ）

1. Write in katakana. （ア～ソ）

so（ ）	e（ ）	ka（ ）
shi（ ）	ke（ ）	sa（ ）
ki（ ）	i（ ）	su（ ）
se（ ）	ko（ ）	u（ ）
a（ ）	ku（ ）	o（ ）

2. Write in katakana. （タ～ホ）

na（ ）	chi（ ）	ni（ ）
hi（ ）	tsu（ ）	ha（ ）
he（ ）	ne（ ）	ta（ ）
no（ ）	te（ ）	nu（ ）
fu（ ）	ho（ ）	to（ ）

3. Write in katakana. （マ～ン）

n（ ）	re（ ）	mi（ ）
yu（ ）	mu（ ）	ya（ ）
me（ ）	ri（ ）	wa（ ）
ra（ ）	ma（ ）	yo（ ）
mo（ ）	ro（ ）	ru（ ）

れんしゅう　5

なまえ（　　　　　　　　　　　）

Look at the pictures and write their names in katakana.

(1)

(2)

(3)

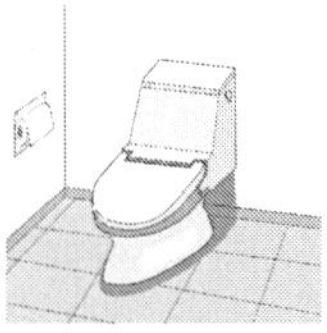

(4)

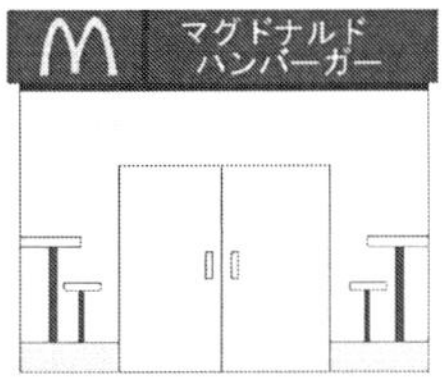

(5)

(6)

(7)

(8)

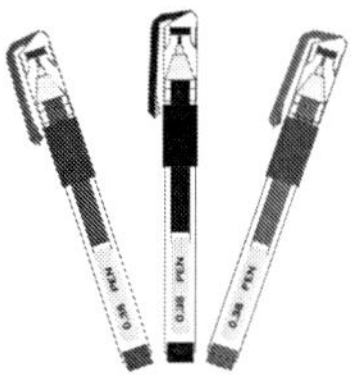

(9)

(10)

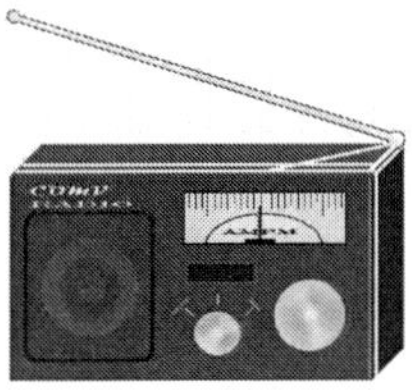

(11)

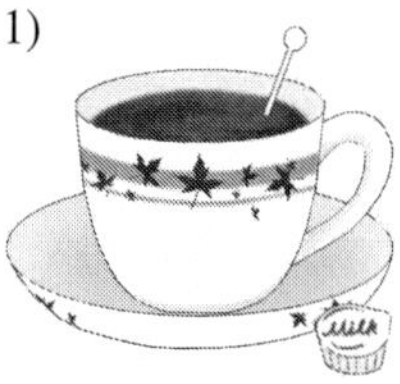

(12)

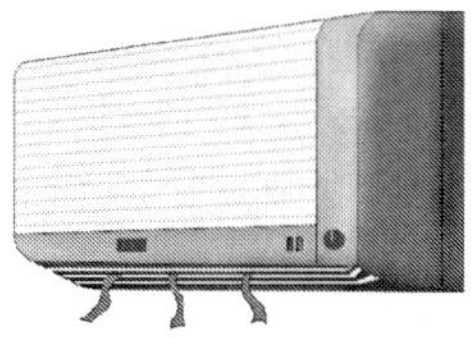

(13)

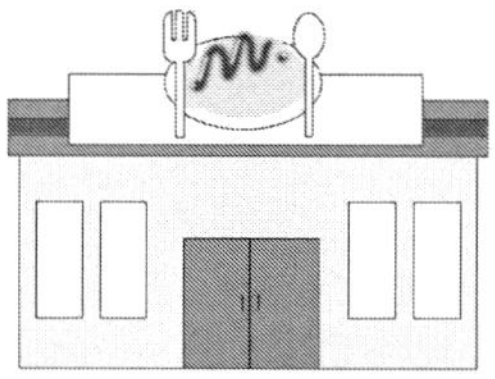

(14)

(15)

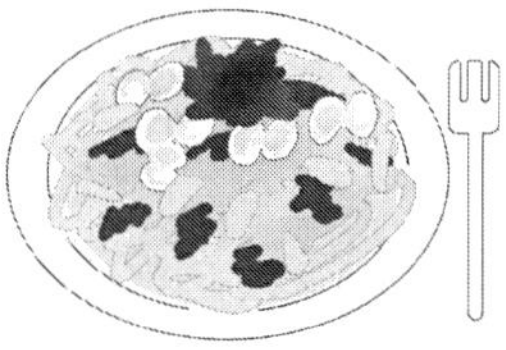

(16)

(17)

(18)

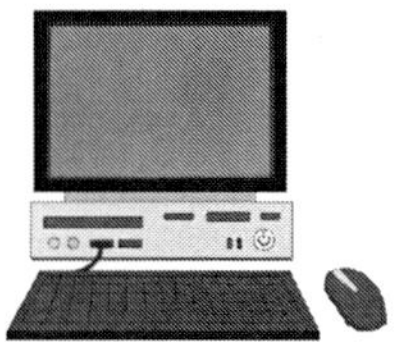

(19)

(20)

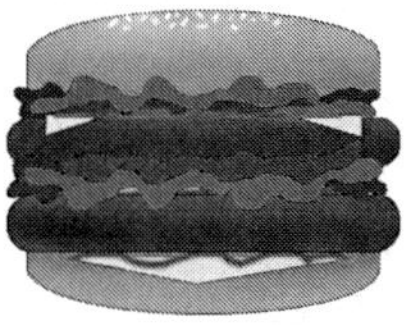

(21)